500

mexican dishes

500
mexican dishes

the only compendium of mexican dishes you'll ever need

Judith Fertig

SELLERS

PUBLISHING

A Quintet Book

Published by Sellers Publishing, Inc.

161 John Roberts Road, South Portland, Maine 04106
For ordering information:
(800) 625-3386 Toll Free
(207) 772-6814 Fax
Visit our Web site: www.sellerspublishing.com
E-mail: rsp@rsvp.com

ISBN: 978-1-4162-0787-0
Library of Congress Control Number: 2009932058
QTT.THME

This book was conceived, designed, and produced by
Quintet Publishing Limited
6 Blundell Street
London N7 9BH
United Kingdom

Project Editor: Asha Savjani
Series Editor: Robert Davies
Editorial Assistants: Camilla Barton, Tanya Laughton
Food Stylist: Fergal Connolly
Photographer: Ian Garlick
Designer: Gavin Edwards
Art Director: Michael Charles
Managing Editor: Donna Gregory
Publisher: James Tavendale

10 9 8 7 6 5 4 3 2 1

Printed in China by 1010 Printing International Ltd.

Shutterstock images appear on pages 13; 168; 227; 253; 277.
Stock Food images appear on pages 73 Andrew Scrivani; 103, 114 Susie M. Eising; 115 Mary Ellen Bartley; 133 Foodcollection; 167 Michael Brauner; 194 Foodcollection; 195 Food Image Source/John Kelly; 218 Andre Baranowski; 223 Valerie Janssen; 226 Ellen Silverman; 250 Bernhard Winkelmann; 276 Allison Dinner; 281 Anita Oberhauser.
Alamy images appear on page 224 © Tim Hill/Alamy.

Quintet Publishing Limited wishes to thank The Mariposa Collection at Casa Mexico (www.casamexico.co.uk).

contents

introduction

The Conquest of Mexico in 1521 gave rise to one of the richest culinary revolutions in history. When the Spanish explorer Hernán Cortéz and his conquistadors came to the Americas in search of gold, they found instead a wealth of New World foods: chocolate, peanuts, vanilla, beans, squash, chiles, avocados, coconuts, guavas, pineapple, prickly pear cactus, corn, and tomatoes.

The ancient Maya (800 BCE to 800 CE), whose homeland stretched from the Yucatán Peninsula on the Caribbean coast westward to the Pacific in southern Mexico, had cultivated the "Three Sisters" of corn, beans, and squash. The Aztecs, who ruled central Mexico from the 1300s until the Conquest, added chocolate, vanilla, coffee, pulque (later transformed into tequila), and chiles. In turn the Spanish brought pork, beef, lamb, citrus fruits, garlic, cheese, milk, wheat, vinegar, and wine. Although the conquistadores systematically destroyed the Aztec empire and replaced it with Spanish ways, they never succeeded in extinguishing the native culture and traditions.

Food, as always, is the conduit from the past to the present. Mexican cooking today starts with ingredients that ancient peoples would have grown or gathered, raised, or hunted. Ancient recipes, such as banana-leaf wrapped meats and fish, pozole, pulque, chocolate drinks, and corn tortillas, are still made in Mexican kitchens. Add to that the European influences from Spanish and French colonials, and you have a vibrant culinary tradition. From the simplest family meal to a high-style dinner, Mexican food still means a fiesta of flavors, textures, and colors.

regional cuisines

A land of great geographical contrasts, Mexico ranges from desert and prairie to lush valleys, coastal lowlands, rugged sierras, and tropical rainforests.

baja
This long peninsula just south of California is famous for its fish tacos and seafood dishes.

chihuahua
The plains of northern Mexico produce wheat, cattle, and dairy products, such as the crumbly white Chihuahua cheese. Tex-Mex dishes heavy on meat and beans are popular here.

durango
The "Wild West" of Mexico is a mountainous region in the north-central part of the country, known for its pine forests, wild game dishes, and queso asadero (a melting-type cheese).

jalisco
Blue agave reigns in this dry region of western Mexico, where the best tequila is made.

oaxaca
Coffee is grown in this southern region and is usually prepared a la olla — laced with sugar and cinnamon and left to simmer in a large pot for hours.

puebla
Just two hours south of Mexico City, Puebla is where the first mole sauce was prepared. Today, every household has its own special version.

sonora

This northwestern region is famous for its wheat flour tortillas, guava cooked down into a fruit paste, prickly pear and nopal, and tamales.

veracruz

In seaside Veracruz, fish is the most popular dish. Any fish dish a la Veracruzana means it is topped with a sauce of tomatoes, olives, capers, and chiles (above).

yucatán

The ancient land of the Maya on the Caribbean coast features foods marinated in achiote (a red annatto paste), then wrapped in banana leaves and cooked outdoors.

ingredients

In Mexico, with its warm climate and long growing season, the cooking relies on fresh, local ingredients, usually grown in small plots by the householder or purchased at the mercado (market). Fresh ingredients round out the staples of the ancient cuisine built upon corn and beans, which are often used dried. With larger families, there is always someone in the kitchen to make a salsa, corn tortillas, a salad, or a sweet treat.

Flavorings such as herbs and chiles help the taste of a dish, but they also add practical nutrients. Herbs such as epazote not only add flavor but also help counter the digestive effects of beans. Chiles contribute a fiery note to bland foods as well as necessary vitamin C. Meat, fish, and chicken are preferably local and used sparingly; that's why you'll find fajitas or strips of grilled meat served with tortillas and condiments rather than a big American steak.

Happily, many supermarkets and grocery stores outside of Mexico now include an expanded section of Hispanic products, where you can find evaporated goat's milk for cajeta, prepared dulce de leche, Mexican chocolate, dried epazote, canned chiles, salsas, dried beans, and much more. In the produce aisle, fresh chiles, avocados, and cilantro are as easy to find as peas, beans, and parsley, while tortillas have become so common that children today have no concept of their country of origin.

beans
Used both fresh and dried. The most common Mexican beans are black beans and pintos. Small beans are often served refrito (refried in lard) or de la olla (simmered in broth).

cactus

A spiky desert plant used as a fruit, vegetable, and base for making tequila. Nopales or cactus pads are boiled, then used in salads and side dishes. Prickly pear fruits are made into jams, jellies, and syrups. Blue agave piñas or fruits go into the production of tequila.

cheese & dairy

These are used mainly for finishing a dish. Queso fresco is a crumbly, white cow's milk cheese; aged queso fresco is called anejo. Queso blanco or Monterey Jack cheese is mild and meltable. Chihuahua is similar to mild cheddar. Queso quesadilla and asadero, mozzarella-like cheeses, are used as a filling for quesadillas. Cotija is an aged, hard grating cheese similar to Parmesan and mainly used to garnish vegetable dishes. Crèma is Mexican-style crème fraîche, a blend of sour cream and cream.

chiles

Used both fresh and dried to add flavor, color, and contrast to bland foods. Even if used fresh, many chiles like poblanos are roasted before using in a recipe (see page 14). Fresh chiles include: Anaheim, guajillo, habañero, jalapeño, New Mexico, poblano, and serrano. Dried chiles include ancho, cascabel, chile negro, and chipotle. Dried chiles are usually soaked in water to soften before using or are ground into a powder as a seasoning. Chiles offer a variety of heat, from the milder Hatch, New Mexico, and jalapeño to the medium-heat poblano/ancho to the hotter-than-hot habañero. Start with jalapeño and move up the chile chain to reach your level of hotness.

herbs

Fresh or dried epazote, similar to oregano, and fresh cilantro are used in many dishes. Epazote helps counter the digestive effects of beans and other ingredients, while cilantro adds a fresh, herby note and green garnish that rounds out the flavor of cheese and chiles.

corn

Used fresh and dried. Corn masa is a flour made from corn kernels soaked in lime and dried (pozole), then ground into flour for corn tortillas and tamales. Instant corn masa flour is the variety most available in American markets and is easiest to use. Dried cornhusks are used to enclose tamales before steaming.

fruits

Mango, papaya, coconut, and pineapple—always plentiful in Mexico because of its warm climate—are eaten fresh as well as in sauces and desserts.

lemons & limes

Key limes, small indigenous fruits, are more sour than the more common, larger Persian limes. Lemons came in with the Spanish. Both fruits thrived in Mexico's mild climate, where their refreshing qualities are welcome in the heat.

piloncillo

Brown, semi-unrefined sugar, formed into a cone and used to sweeten desserts, coffee, and fruit dishes.

seeds

Pepitas or roasted pumpkin seeds and piñons or pine nuts are used in sauces and as a garnish.

tomatoes

Both canned and fresh tomatoes are the essential ingredient for fresh and cooked salsas. Small, tart tomatillos are green tomatoes encased in a papery husk, often used for a green salsa served with chicken and fish.

equipment

Mexican food can be made with the usual indoor kitchen equipment: blender or food processor, chopping board and knives, measuring cups and spoons, pots and pans, garlic press, grater, and wooden spoons. Outdoors, a simple barbecue grill with a lid and barbecue equipment such as grill tongs and spatula are enough to get you started. But if you want to take a very authentic approach to Mexican cuisine, you might want to check out the following:

cazuela

This glazed earthenware pot is used to cook moles, beans, corn, and stews.

comal

This cast-iron grill pan is used to warm tortillas and to make carne asada. You can also use a cast-iron skillet or a ridged grill pan.

metate y mano

With a slightly concave base made of lava rock and a heavy cylinder held in your hand, you grind corn, spices, cacao beans, or other hard ingredients.

molcajete

This mortar and pestle, usually made of stone, is the traditional way to make guacamole. It's also good for mashing garlic or making fresh salsas.

molinillo

This wooden whisk, held between your two palms, is the traditional way to add froth to chocolate beverages.

tortillero

The tortilla press is a hinged, metal gadget. You place a ball of corn tortilla dough on the bottom, then use the lever to press the top down and create a flat tortilla.

vitrolero

Used for aguas frescas, this large glass container with a spout, common in Mexican markets, is also great for lemonade and other cold drinks.

basic recipes

A typical Mexican meal depends on freshly made basic foods—a homemade corn or flour tortilla, a fresh pico de gallo, cactus "nopalitos" made tender and delicious, or crisp fried tortilla chips. The better these basics, the better the overall flavor in the meal. Salsas, or "sauces" in Mexican cuisine, can be made from raw ingredients—cruda—or cooked. However they're made, salsas add a wealth of color, texture, and flavor to even the most simple dish. The blend of fresh herbs and spices makes each different salsa dish unique.

roasted chiles

Chiles are used, both fresh and dried, in many dishes. But even when used fresh, many chiles are roasted before using in a recipe. To roast a fresh chile, hold it with a long-handled fork over a gas flame, place it on a baking sheet under the broiler, or put it in a barbecue grill. Turn the chile until it is blackened and blistered all over. Place the roasted chile in a sealable plastic bag, close the bag, and let it steam for 5 minutes. Remove the skin under cold, running water. Then remove the stems and seeds and chop the chile.

Be careful when handling fresh chiles. The seeds and membranes contain 80 percent of the chile's heat-producing capsaicin, so wear food-handler's gloves as you work with them or wash your hands thoroughly after chopping and removing the seeds and membranes.

pico de gallo

This "rooster's beak" fresh garnish is a must-have with tacos, burritos, and even slow-simmered dishes. It got its name from the tradition of picking up the raw garnish with thumb and forefinger, a shape that resembles a rooster beak pecking the ground.

3 plum tomatoes, chopped
1/2 small red onion, chopped
1/4 cup fresh lime juice

2 tbsp. chopped fresh cilantro
2 tbsp. chopped fresh jalapeño pepper
1 1/2 tsp. salt

Stir all ingredients together. Serve at room temperature. Makes about 1 1/2 cups.

soft corn tortillas

The Aztecs called their flat griddle cakes made with ground hominy flour tlaxcalli. The Spanish conquistadores renamed them "tortillas" after the round cake they knew in Spain. Whatever you call them, freshly made corn tortillas are delicious. Use a tortilla press to make these traditional accompaniments to any Mexican meal.

2 cups instant corn masa flour
1/4 tsp. salt

1 1/4 cups warm water, or more if necessary

Place the masa flour and salt in a bowl. Stir in the water to make a soft dough, adding a little more water if necessary. Divide the dough into 16 portions and form each portion into a ball. Cover with a damp cloth to keep the dough moist. Place each ball of dough between two unopened plastic sandwich bags, then press to a 5- to 6-inch round in a tortilla press. Preheat an ungreased skillet over medium-high heat. Cook each tortilla for 1 minute on each side or until golden in spots. Cover with a damp tea towel until ready to serve. Makes 16 (5- to 6-inch) tortillas.

fried tortilla chips

Freshly made soft corn tortillas are delicious to serve warm, but they're not as easy to make into fried tortilla chips as corn tortillas are, as they have more moisture than the manufactured kind. So use your favorite store-bought corn tortilla to make these chips. Serve with salsa or bake with shredded cheeses, chiles, onion, and cilantro for nachos.

12 (6-inch) corn tortillas
vegetable oil for frying

salt

On a flat surface, stack 4 tortillas on top of each other, making 3 stacks of tortillas. Using a pizza wheel or a sharp knife, slice each tortilla stack into 8 triangles. In a deep fryer or a large, deep skillet, heat 2 inches of vegetable oil to 350°F. Fry the triangles in batches until golden brown and crisp, about 30-60 seconds. Remove with a slotted spoon, drain on paper towels, and salt to taste. Serve right away or store in an airtight container at room temperature for up to 2 days. Makes 8 dozen.

homemade flour tortillas

Spanish settlers to Mexico brought wheat flour with them, which was then made into a version of the corn tortilla. Homemade flour tortillas, hot off the griddle, taste wonderful and can be used for quesadillas, burritos, and more.

3 cups all-purpose flour
2 tsp. baking powder

3/4 tsp. salt
1 cup warm water, or more if necessary

Place the flour, baking powder, and salt in a bowl. Stir in the water to make a soft dough, adding a little more water if necessary. Divide the dough into 12 portions and form each

portion into a ball. Cover with a damp cloth to keep the dough moist and let rest for
15 minutes. Roll out each ball of dough on a floured surface to a 9-inch-diameter round.
Heat an ungreased skillet over medium-high heat. Cook each tortilla for 1 minute per side,
pressing down with a spatula for several seconds, or until browned and blistered in spots.
Remove from the pan and start cooking the next tortilla. Stack the cooked tortillas on top of
each other, cover with a tea towel, and place in a sealable plastic bag to steam until ready to
serve. Makes 12 (9-inch) tortillas.

nopalitos

Nopales or pads of prickly pear cactus become integral parts of soups, salsas, and salads
when they're carefully trimmed of their prickly spines and cooked. When these pads are
sliced into strips, they become nopalitos. You'll find fresh nopales at Hispanic markets.

1 lb. fresh nopales

**1 fresh jalapeño or serrano pepper, stemmed and
seeded**

Holding the cactus pads with oven mitts or a towel, slice off the prickly spines and the
thorny edge of the pad. If necessary, peel the cactus pad. Cut the trimmed pad into
1/4-inch-wide strips. Bring a large pot of water to a boil over high heat. Add the sliced
cactus strips and the whole chile. Cook, uncovered, until the cactus is tender when pricked
with a knife, about 7–8 minutes. Drain, rinse with cold water, and use right away or keep
covered in the refrigerator for up to 5 days. Makes about 2 cups.

basic mole

Mole, a sauce made from many different ground ingredients, comes from the word molli
meaning "concoction." Legend has it that the first mole was served at a convent in the

central Mexican town of Puebla de Los Angeles as a special dish for a visiting dignitary. Today, every household has its own version of mole (and you can find many different varieties at the supermarket), but all agree that mole tastes best with poultry—from the indigenous Mexican turkey known as gaujolote, to domestic turkey, chicken, or Cornish game hen. Moles usually contain a variety of ground chiles, roasted nuts or seeds, green plantain, and a hint of chocolate to deepen the flavor.

2 tbsp. ground dried ancho chile
1 cup whole blanched almonds
1/4 cup diced green plantain
1 tsp. ground cinnamon
1 clove garlic
2 soft corn tortillas (homemade or bought), torn
    into pieces

2 tbsp. roasted pumpkin seeds
1/2 (3.3-ounce) disk Mexican chocolate or
    1 oz. semisweet chocolate
2 cups chicken broth
1/2 cup chopped canned tomatoes, with juice
salt to taste

In a blender or food processor, grind the chile powder, almonds, plantain, cinnamon, garlic, tortilla pieces, pumpkin seeds, and chocolate with 1 cup of the chicken broth until puréed but grainy. Pour the mixture into a saucepan, add the remaining 1 cup chicken broth and tomatoes, and bring to a simmer, stirring, over medium heat. Cook, stirring, until the chocolate melts and the flavors have blended, about 5 minutes. Season with salt to taste. Serve as a cooking or finishing sauce with poultry. Will keep, chilled, for up to 3 days. Makes about 2 cups.

basic mole variations

yellow mole: Instead of the basic recipe, in a blender or food processor, process 15 guajillo or Amarillo chiles, roasted, stemmed, deveined, and seeded; 1 (13-oz.) can tomatillos with liquid; 2 cloves minced garlic; 1/2 teaspoon ground cumin; 1/2 teaspoon dried oregano; and

1/2 teaspoon ground cinnamon, until smooth. Season to taste with salt and pepper. Bring to a boil over medium-high heat, reduce heat, and simmer 15 minutes to let flavors blend.

green mole: Instead of the basic recipe, purée 2 (13-oz.) cans tomatillos, 1 cup finely chopped onion, 1/4 cup toasted almonds, 1 tablespoon freshly chopped cilantro, and 3 tablespoons diced green chiles in a food processor or blender. Season to taste with salt and pepper.

doctored-up mole: Instead of the basic recipe, start with a store-bought mole. Doctor the mole with bottled smoked chipotle sauce, chopped garlic, honey, and/or chopped fresh cilantro, to taste.

tomatillo salsa

Tart, tangy, and pale green, tomatillo salsa is usually served with chicken, pork, or fish. Tomatillos, smaller and greener cousins of the red beefsteak tomato, have papery husks that enclose the small fruits; remove the husks before using.

1 1/2 lbs fresh tomatillos
1/2 cup chopped fresh cilantro
1/3 cup fresh lime juice

salt to taste
1 jalapeño pepper, stemmed and seeded

Remove the husks from the tomatillos and discard. Arrange the tomatillos on a baking sheet in a single layer and roast in a 450°F oven until lightly browned (about 20 minutes). Let cool. In a blender or food processor, place the cooled tomatillos, cilantro, jalapeño, and lime juice. Process until somewhat smooth. Add salt to taste. Will keep, covered, in the refrigerator for up to 3 days. Makes about 2 cups.

tomatillo salsa variations

green tomato salsa: Prepare the basic recipe, using the same quantity of fresh, small, green tomatoes, cored, in place of tomatillos. Add sugar to taste.

pantry shelf tomatillo salsa: Prepare the basic recipe, using 1 1/2 cups canned tomatillos and 1 (4-oz.) can chopped jalapeño in place of the fresh tomatillos and jalapeño. Just stir in the cilantro, lime juice, and salt to taste.

grilled tomatillo salsa: Prepare the basic recipe, but instead of roasting the tomatillos, husk them, brush with olive oil, and grill over medium-high heat, turning often, until they have good grill marks.

poblano tomatillo salsa: Prepare the basic recipe, using a fresh poblano in place of the jalapeño.

pineapple salsa

Golden and tangy fresh pineapple salsa is delicious with fish and shellfish, chicken, and pork dishes. Try it on grilled chicken tacos and fish tostadas, or alongside pork carnitas.

2 cups chopped fresh pineapple
1/2 cup chopped fresh cilantro
1 fresh jalapeño pepper, stemmed and seeded

1/2 tsp. crushed red pepper flakes
salt

Place the pineapple, cilantro, jalapeño pepper, and red pepper flakes in a blender or food processor. Process until somewhat smooth. Add salt to taste. Will keep, covered, in the refrigerator for up to 3 days. Makes about 2 1/2 cups.

pineapple salsa variations

pantry shelf pineapple salsa: Prepare the basic recipe, using canned pineapple in fruit juice, drained, in place of fresh pineapple. Add sugar to taste.

papaya salsa: Prepare the basic recipe, using fresh sliced papaya in place of fresh pineapple. Add a little lime juice to taste.

mango salsa: Prepare the basic recipe, using fresh sliced mango in place of fresh pineapple. Add a little lime juice to taste.

strawberry & pineapple salsa: Prepare the basic recipe, using 1 cup hulled and sliced fresh strawberries in place of 1 cup of the pineapple.

salsa cruda

Made from raw, fresh ingredients, this salsa is perfect with tortilla chips and a frosty margarita or a Mexican beer.

2 cloves garlic, minced
1/4 cup finely chopped onion
1/2 cup grated fresh jicama
1/2 cup finely chopped cucumber
1/4 cup chopped fresh cilantro
1 lb. firm, ripe tomatoes, stemmed and chopped

juice of 2 limes
1 fresh jalapeño pepper, stemmed, seeded, and finely chopped salt and pepper

Combine all ingredients in a bowl. Season to taste and let sit at room temperature until ready to serve. Makes about 2 cups.

salsa cruda variations

frozen salsa cruda: Prepare the basic recipe. Freeze the salsa in a metal bowl, stirring every 30 minutes, until slushy, about 4 hours. Serve with chilled, cooked shrimp or oysters on the half-shell.

golden salsa cruda: Prepare the basic recipe, using yellow tomatoes in place of the red tomatoes and yellow bell pepper in place of jalapeño. Add 1/2 teaspoon ground chipotle.

cherry tomato salsa cruda: Prepare the basic recipe, using halved cherry tomatoes in place of the red tomatoes.

mixed tomato salsa cruda: Prepare the basic recipe, using an assortment of fresh tomatoes in place of the red tomatoes.

mango & lime salsa

Tropical mangoes and the small Key limes of coastal Mexico combine to make a fresh salsa that is delicious with grilled fish and shellfish.

2 cloves garlic, minced
1/4 cup finely chopped onion
1 jalapeño pepper, stemmed, seeded, and
   finely chopped

1/4 cup chopped fresh cilantro
2 cups chopped peeled mango
juice of 1 Persian lime or 2 Key limes
salt and pepper to taste

Combine all ingredients in a bowl. Season to taste and let sit at room temperature until ready to serve. Will keep, covered, in the refrigerator for up to 3 days. Let come to room temperature before serving.

mango & lime salsa variations

frozen mango & lime salsa: Prepare the basic recipe. Freeze the salsa in a metal bowl, stirring every 30 minutes, until slushy, about 4 hours.

papaya & lime salsa: Prepare the basic recipe, using fresh chopped papaya in place of the mango.

pineapple, mango & lime salsa: Prepare the basic recipe, using 1 cup chopped fresh pineapple in place of 1 cup of the chopped mango.

mango & orange salsa: Prepare the basic recipe, adding 1 cup chopped orange to the ingredients.

salsa roja

Salsa roja, or red salsa from Mexico City, is a cooked version most often served with enchiladas. It's also delicious drizzled on eggs, quesadillas, or steak.

6 large, ripe tomatoes
3 serrano chiles
3 tbsp. chicken bouillon powder
2 tbsp. olive oil
3 cloves garlic, minced
1/4 cup chopped onion
salt to taste

Place the tomatoes and serrano chiles in a medium saucepan with enough water to cover. Bring to a boil. Reduce the heat and simmer until the tomato skins are peeling off and the tomatoes are soft but not mushy, about 5 minutes. Remove 1/2 cup of the hot cooking water and whisk it with the chicken bouillon in a small bowl until completely dissolved. Remove the tomatoes and chiles with a slotted spoon and let cool for a few minutes, then peel off the tomato skins and stem and seed the chiles. Place the bouillon mixture, peeled tomatoes, and seeded chiles in a blender or food processor, and pulse to process for just a few seconds until blended but still chunky. Heat the olive oil in a large sauté pan over medium-high heat, then sauté the garlic and onion until softened, about 2 minutes. Stir in the tomato mixture and cook, stirring, until the liquid has evaporated and the sauce has thickened (about 6–8 minutes). Season to taste and serve hot. Makes about 3 cups.

salsa roja variations

chunky pantry shelf salsa roja: Prepare the basic recipe, using 1 cup canned chopped plum tomatoes with liquid in place of the fresh tomatoes and 1 (4 oz.) can jalapeño in place of serrano chiles. Mix them with the bouillon concentrate that's been dissolved in 1/2 cup hot water and proceed with the recipe.

grilled tomato salsa roja: Prepare the basic recipe, but instead of boiling the tomatoes and serrano chiles, grill them until you have good grill marks and the skins are papery. Remove their skins, stems, and seeds and finely chop. Instead of the tomato-boiling water, use 1/2 cup hot water, and proceed with the recipe.

salsa d'oro: Prepare the basic recipe, using 6 medium yellow tomatoes in place of the 6 red tomatoes and 1 large yellow bell pepper in place of the serrano chiles. Add 1/2 teaspoon ground dried chipotle and proceed with the recipe.

easy salsa roja: Prepare the basic recipe, using 2 cups canned tomato purée in place of fresh tomatoes. Seed, stem, and chop serrano chile, and sauté with the onion and garlic. Add the tomato purée and salt to taste, cooking until somewhat thickened.

pumpkin seed salsa

Made with pepitas (toasted pumpkin seeds), this salsa has a pleasant "toasty" flavor that goes well with grilled foods.

1 cup toasted pumpkin seeds
2 cloves garlic
zest and juice of 1 lime
1 cup chopped fresh cilantro

1/4 cup olive oil
1 1/2 cups canned diced tomatoes with
  green chiles

Place all ingredients in a blender or food processor and purée until almost smooth. Keep at room temperature until ready to serve. Makes about 2 cups.

pumpkin seed salsa variations

double pumpkin seed salsa: Prepare the basic recipe, using 3/4 cup canned pumpkin in place of 3/4 cup of the canned tomatoes with green chiles.

doctored-up pumpkin seed salsa: Instead of the basic recipe, blend 1/2 cup toasted pumpkin seeds with 1 cup store-bought pipian (a pumpkin seed mole). Add olive oil, lime juice, canned tomatoes with green chiles, and chopped fresh cilantro to taste.

spanish almond salsa: Prepare the basic recipe, using toasted sliced almonds in place of pumpkin seeds. Toast 1 cup sliced almonds on a baking sheet in a 350°F oven until lightly browned; let cool.

cilantro salsa

Vividly green and sharp-tasting, this salsa perks up grilled and slow-simmered foods like chicken, pork, fish, and shellfish, as well as basic nachos or a plain grilled cheese.

1/2 cup chopped green onion
1 cup chopped fresh cilantro
1/2 cup chopped fresh Italian parsley
1/2 cup vegetable oil

6 tbsp. freshly squeezed lime juice
3 tbsp. white vinegar
2 cloves garlic, minced
1/4 cup chopped jalapeño pepper

Combine all ingredients together in a bowl. Serve right away.

cilantro salsa variations

fennel & tarragon salsa: Prepare the basic recipe, using chopped fresh bulb fennel in place of the cilantro and tarragon vinegar in place of the white vinegar.

grilled onion salsa with sherry vinegar: Prepare the basic recipe, using a grilled large red onion in place of the green onions and sherry vinegar in place of the white vinegar. To grill the onion, grill slices on both sides, then chop fine.

orange & cilantro salsa: Prepare the basic recipe, adding 1 cup peeled sliced orange to the ingredients.

lemon–parsley salsa: Prepare the basic recipe, using Italian parsley in place of the cilantro and lemon juice in place of lime juice.

mango cream

Wonderful with lobster-papaya quesadillas (page 34), this multipurpose sauce is also good on simple grilled chicken breasts or fish fillets. For extra color and flavor, use mango salsa (page 21) as a garnish.

2 ripe mangoes, peeled and pitted   **fresh lemon juice to taste**
1/2 cup Mexican crèma or sour cream

Place the mangoes, sour cream, and lemon juice in a food processor or blender and purée until smooth. Use right away or cover and refrigerate for up to 2 days.

mango cream variations

papaya cream: Prepare the basic recipe, using fresh papaya in place of the mango.

sweet mango cream: Transform this into a dessert sauce by using heavy cream in place of sour cream and lime juice instead of lemon juice. Add a little sugar to taste.

mango & lime cream: Prepare the basic recipe, using freshly grated lime zest and fresh lime juice in place of lemon juice.

mango & orange cream: Prepare the basic recipe, using freshly grated orange zest and fresh orange juice in place of lemon juice.

antojitos

Antojitos ("little whims") are nibbled throughout

the day. They can be called snacks or appetizers, but

they must be delicious.

queso al horno with tortilla chips

see variations page 43

This baked cheese appetizer is easy to assemble and delicious to eat.

1 1/2 tbsp. vegetable oil
1 large onion, chopped
2 fresh, large tomatoes, peeled, seeded, and
   coarsely chopped
4–6 fresh jalapeño peppers, stemmed, seeded,
   and diced

1/4 tsp. ground dried chipotle chile
salt to taste
2 lbs. grated Monterey Jack cheese
1 small, whole jalapeño pepper, to garnish
tortilla chips, for serving

Heat the oil in a skillet over a medium-high heat. Sauté the onion until softened, stirring occasionally, for about 10 minutes. Add the tomatoes and jalapeños and cook, stirring, until the peppers have softened, about 2 more minutes. Season to taste with ground dried chipotle and salt.

Preheat oven to 350°F. Place the grated cheese in an 8- to 10-inch round baking dish at least 1 1/2 inches deep. Spoon the tomato mixture onto the middle of the cheese, then spread the tomato mixture to a 6-inch diameter. Bake the cheese for 25–30 minutes or until bubbling. Garnish the center with the whole jalapeño. Serve hot with tortilla chips.

Serves 12

authentic guacamole

see variations page 44

Made with ripe, buttery avocados and tart lime juice, guacamole also has a bit of heat from chiles. For the most authentic preparation and presentation, use a molcajete — a stone mortar and pestle. When you make guacamole, you should serve it right away, as it can discolor as it sits.

2 large, ripe avocados
3 tbsp. fresh lime juice
2 tbsp. finely chopped fresh cilantro
2 fresh jalapeño peppers, stemmed, seeded, and
    finely chopped

Halve, pit, peel, and slice the avocados into a molcajete or a bowl. With the pestle of the molcajete or a fork, mash the avocados with the lime juice, cilantro, and jalapeño until chunky but well blended. Serve with tortilla chips or use as a garnish for other dishes.

Makes about 1 1/2 cups

market day tortas

see variations page 45

A torta in Mexico is a sandwich — usually with a meat and bean filling — on a crusty roll known as a bolillo. Street vendors often serve tortas to busy shoppers on market days, but they're just as tasty for a casual meal at home.

4 rectangular bolillos or crusty rolls, about
   6-8 inches long
2 tbsp. butter
3/4 lb. chorizo sausage, casings removed
1 large onion, thinly sliced
1 (15-oz.) can pinto beans, drained, or 2 cups
   frijoles refritos (page 209)

3/4 cup crèma or heavy cream
8 oz. shredded Chihuahua or Monterey Jack
   cheese
4 tbsp. tomatillo salsa (page 19)

Slice the rolls lengthwise and butter the cut sides. Place rolls, cut-side down, in a large skillet over medium-high heat, and let brown. Remove and reserve, keeping them warm. Cook the chorizo, stirring, until well browned, about 10 minutes. Remove with a slotted spoon and reserve. Remove all but 3 tablespoons of fat from the pan, then cook the onion, stirring, until lightly browned, about 7 minutes. Stir in the beans, mashing well. Stir in the crèma and reserved chorizo and cook until bubbling.

Spoon the chorizo filling onto the bottoms of the rolls. Sprinkle each with a quarter of the cheese and 1 tablespoon of salsa and serve.

Serves 4

gulf coast ceviche

see variations page 46

Originating in Peru centuries ago, ceviche traveled northward to Mexico, where it has become part of the coastal diet. Small pieces of fish and shellfish are "cooked" with tangy lime juice to make a refreshing appetizer during warm months. If you like, serve ceviche in cocktail glasses or little bowls.

12 oz. fresh swordfish, tuna, or mahi mahi cut
    into small cubes
1/2 cup fresh lime juice
2 tbsp. fresh orange juice
1 tsp. ground cumin
1 tsp. ground dried ancho chile
salt and ground white pepper to taste

1 cup seeded and finely chopped watermelon
1/2 cup freshly grated jicama
1/2 cup finely chopped green onion
1/2 cup finely chopped and peeled ripe tomato

Put the fish in a large glass or ceramic bowl. Add the lime and orange juices, cumin, ancho chile, salt, and white pepper. Mix well and cover tightly with plastic wrap. Refrigerate for 15 minutes.

Unwrap, then stir in the watermelon, jicama, onion, and tomato. Cover tightly again and refrigerate for 15 more minutes or until the fish is turning opaque on the outside but is still rare on the inside. Serve chilled.

Serves 8

lobster-papaya quesadillas with mango cream

see variations page 47

Served with a frosty margarita or a glass of chilled white wine, nothing could be finer. Papayas and mangoes from the tropical coasts of Mexico add an exotic flair to the traditional quesadilla appetizer.

4 oz. fresh goat cheese, crumbled
1 garlic clove, crushed
1/4 cup chopped onion
1/2 poblano chile, roasted, stemmed, peeled, seeded, and diced
1/2 red bell pepper, roasted, peeled, seeded, and diced
2 tsp. minced fresh cilantro

1/4 tsp. salt
2 tsp. fresh lime juice
1 cup cooked and chopped lobster meat
1 papaya, peeled, seeded, and chopped
4 (6-inch) flour tortillas (store-bought or homemade)
2 tbsp. unsalted butter
mango cream (page 27), for serving

In a large bowl, combine the goat cheese, garlic, onion, peppers, cilantro, salt, and lime juice. Carefully blend in the lobster and papaya. Spread some lobster mixture over half of each tortilla and fold over. Brush each tortilla with melted butter.

Heat a large nonstick skillet over medium-high heat. Cook quesadillas for 3–4 minutes, turning once, until browned on both sides. Cut each into triangles and serve with mango cream.

Serves 4

beef salpicon with fresh cilantro & corn tortillas

see variations page 48

Salpicon, which translates as "hodgepodge," is a mixture of cold cooked meats and vegetables with a tangy dressing. It's delicious as a first course and ideal as buffet food.

3 1/2-4 lbs. fully trimmed beef brisket "flat" or boneless chuck roast
1 large onion, chopped
2 bay leaves
3 cloves garlic, minced
2 cups bottled chipotle mojo marinade
1/3 cup canned chipotle peppers in adobo sauce
6 tbsp. extra-virgin olive oil
1/4 cup fresh lime juice
2 tbsp. white vinegar

1 tbsp. minced onion
1 clove garlic, minced
salt and pepper to taste
4 fresh, small plum tomatoes, diced
2 ripe avocados, diced
1 medium red onion, diced
6 oz. Monterey Jack cheese, in small cubes
1/2 cup chopped fresh cilantro, to garnish
soft corn tortillas (page 15), for serving

In a large, heavy pot, place the beef, onion, bay leaves, garlic, and chipotle marinade. Add enough water to cover. Bring to a boil, then reduce the heat and simmer until the meat is tender, about 3–4 hours. Let the meat cool in the pot for 30 minutes. Remove 2 tablespoons of the liquid in the pot and reserve. Discard remaining liquid. Shred the meat and set aside. To make the dressing, place the reserved pot liquid, chipotle peppers, olive oil, lime juice, vinegar, onion, garlic, salt, and pepper in a food processor. Purée until smooth. Mix the shredded meat with three-quarters of the dressing, then toss it lightly with the tomatoes, avocados, onion, and cheese. Drizzle over the remaining dressing. Garnish with chopped cilantro. Serve warm with hot tortillas or chilled with tortilla chips for dipping.

Serves 12

fried plantains with salsa cruda

see variations page 49

Plantains are more starchy and less sweet than bananas, their botanical cousins. In Mexico, plantains are used like potatoes. Ripe plantains are fried in place of potatoes for a breakfast side dish, and green (unripe) plantains are transformed into these potato chip–like tostones. A special wooden tostonera (or the bottom of a drinking glass) is used to flatten these partially cooked plantains.

2 cups vegetable oil
2 green plantains

salt and pepper to taste
salsa cruda (page 21), for serving

In a large frying pan or deep fryer, heat the oil to about 350°F. Peel and slice the plantains into 1-inch rounds. Place them in the hot oil and cook for about 3 minutes while turning. Remove from oil and pat dry with a paper towel. Place each round inside a plastic sandwich bag and flatten it with the bottom of a drinking glass or a tostonera. Return the plantains to the hot oil for about 3 more minutes, turning, until golden brown on both sides. Transfer to paper towels and pat dry. Season to taste. Serve with salsa cruda (or with authentic guacamole, page 30, if preferred).

Serves 4

chile-spiced peanuts

see variations page 50

These spicy cacahuates or peanut snacks from Oaxaca can be addictive. They're great with a cold Mexican beer. Make a big batch and store in an airtight container to have on hand.

15–20 small, dried, whole red chiles
4 cloves garlic, minced
3 tbsp. vegetable oil

2 lbs. roasted salted peanuts
1 tsp. coarse kosher salt
1 tsp. ground dried ancho or chipotle chile

In a large skillet, combine the chiles, garlic, and oil. Cook over medium heat, stirring, for 1 minute. Add the peanuts and cook, stirring, until slightly browned and very fragrant, about 5 minutes. Remove from the heat and season with salt and ground ancho or chipotle chile, stirring well. Let cool, then store in an airtight container.

Makes about 7 cups

empanadas

see variations page 51

These small turnovers with their savory picadillo filling (with a touch of sweetness) are great as appetizers or snacks. Use ready-made discos grandes (frozen rounds of empanada dough) or prepared pie dough for the pastry.

1 package discos grandes (about 10), frozen and
    thawed, or 2 prepared pie pastry rounds
1 lb. ground beef
1 clove garlic, minced

1/2 cup canned tomato purée
1/2 cup golden raisins
1/2 cup chopped pimiento-stuffed green olives
vegetable oil for frying

In a large skillet, brown the ground beef and garlic together. Stir in the tomato purée, raisins, and olives. Set aside to cool.

Lay each disc of empanada dough on a flat surface or use a 3-inch biscuit cutter to cut out rounds from the prepared pie dough. Spoon the filling into the center of each round. Moisten the edges of the dough with water and fold in half, crimping the edges closed with a fork.

Heat vegetable oil in a large skillet and fry the empanadas, turning once, until golden brown on both sides, about 2 minutes total. Transfer to paper towels to drain. Serve warm.

Serves 10–12

queso al horno with tortilla chips

see base recipe page 29

vegetarian baked cheese with chiles
Prepare the basic recipe, using vegetarian cheese in place of Monterey Jack.

baked cheese with chicken & chiles
Prepare the basic recipe, topping the tomato mixture with 1 cup finely chopped cooked chicken before garnishing with the whole jalapeño.

baked cheese with pork carnitas & chiles
Prepare the basic recipe, topping the tomato mixture with 1 cup finely chopped pork carnitas (page 143) before garnishing with the whole jalapeño.

baked cheese with chorizo & chiles
Prepare the basic recipe, topping the tomato mixture with 1 cup cooked and crumbled chorizo sausage before garnishing with the whole jalapeño.

authentic guacamole

see base recipe page 30

grilled guacamole

Halve and pit the avocados, but do not peel. Grill the avocado halves,
cut-side down, outside on a medium-hot barbecue grill or indoors on a grill
pan for 2–3 minutes or until you have good grill marks. Proceed with the
basic recipe.

smoky tomato guacamole

Prepare the basic recipe, adding 1 cup chopped fresh tomato and 1 teaspoon
liquid smoke.

fresh guacamole with lime & garlic

Prepare the basic recipe, adding 1 teaspoon minced garlic and 1 more
tablespoon fresh lime juice.

easy guacamole

Halve and pit the avocados. Scoop the flesh into a bowl, drizzle with the
juice of 1 lime, mash with a fork, and add salt to taste.

variations

market day tortas

see base recipe page 31

grilled chicken tortas
Prepare the basic recipe, using chopped grilled chicken in place of the chorizo.

pork carnitas tortas
Prepare the basic recipe, using pork carnitas (page 143) in place of the chorizo.

grilled vegetable & chile tortas
Prepare the basic recipe, using 4 ounces each sliced onion, zucchini, and fresh chiles, grilled, in place of the chorizo.

taco tortas
Prepare the basic recipe, using 3/4 pound ground beef and 1 tablespoon taco seasoning in place of the chorizo. Use a red tomato salsa such as salsa cruda (page 21) in place of the tomatillo salsa.

grilled chicken & avocado tortas
Prepare the basic recipe, using chopped grilled chicken and diced avocado in place of the chorizo and pinto beans.

variations

gulf coast ceviche

see base recipe page 33

fresh tuna ceviche
Prepare the basic recipe, using sashimi-grade tuna, chopped avocado in place of the watermelon, and chopped fresh cilantro in place of the onion.

shrimp chipotle ceviche
Prepare the basic recipe, using 8 raw, peeled and deveined medium-size shrimp, cut into 1/2-inch pieces, in place of the fish; 2 chipotle canned chiles in adobo sauce, chopped, in place of the watermelon; and chopped fresh cilantro in place of the onion.

fresh swordfish-peach ceviche
Prepare the basic recipe, using fresh swordfish, peeled and chopped fresh peaches in place of the watermelon, and chopped fresh cilantro in place of the onion.

lobster, poblano & mango ceviche
Prepare the basic recipe, using 4 fresh or frozen and thawed lobster tails—cooked in boiling water for 3 minutes or until the shells turn red, and then chopped—in place of the fish; 2 pitted and chopped mangoes in place of the watermelon; 1 poblano chile—roasted, stemmed, seeded, and chopped—in place of the tomatos; and chopped fresh cilantro in place of the onion.

lobster-papaya quesadillas with mango cream

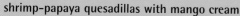

see base recipe page 34

shrimp-papaya quesadillas with mango cream
Prepare the basic recipe, using 1 cup cooked shrimp in place of the lobster.

grilled chicken-papaya quesadillas with mango cream
Prepare the basic recipe, using 1 cup chopped grilled chicken in place of the lobster.

grilled pork-papaya quesadillas with mango cream
Prepare the basic recipe, using 1 cup grilled and chopped pork tenderloin in place of the lobster.

cheese, chile & papaya quesadillas with mango cream
Prepare the basic recipe, using 1 cup shredded Monterey Jack cheese and 1 small seeded and chopped jalapeño in place of the lobster.

variations

beef salpicon with fresh cilantro & corn tortillas

see base recipe page 36

chicken salpicon with fresh cilantro & corn tortillas

Prepare the basic recipe, using a 4-pound roasting chicken in place of brisket.

pork salpicon with fresh cilantro & corn tortillas

Prepare the basic recipe, using a 4-pound boneless pork butt or pork shoulder roast in place of brisket.

lamb salpicon with fresh cilantro & corn tortillas

Prepare the basic recipe, using a 4-pound boneless lamb shoulder roast in place of brisket.

fried plantains with salsa cruda

see base recipe page 38

fried plantains with tomatillo salsa
Prepare the basic recipe, using tomatillo salsa (page 19) instead of salsa cruda.

fried plantains with pineapple salsa
Prepare the basic recipe, using pineapple salsa (page 20) instead of salsa cruda.

fried plantains with papaya salsa
Prepare the basic recipe, using papaya salsa (page 21) instead of salsa cruda.

fried plantains with salsa cruda, black beans & crèma
Prepare the basic recipe, adding 2 cups canned black beans to 1 cup of the salsa cruda. Add a dollop of crèma and serve.

variations

chile-spiced peanuts

see base recipe page 40

chile-spiced mixed nuts
Prepare the basic recipe, using 2 cups mixed nuts in place of peanuts.

chile-spiced pecans
Prepare the basic recipe, using 2 cups pecan halves in place of peanuts.

chile-spiced almonds
Prepare the basic recipe, using 2 cups whole blanched almonds in place
of peanuts.

chile-piloncillo almonds
Prepare the basic recipe, using 2 cups whole blanched almonds in place of
peanuts and adding 1/4 cup finely crumbled piloncillo or brown sugar to the
seasoning at the end.

variations

empanadas

see base recipe page 42

turkey empanadas
Prepare the basic recipe, using ground turkey in place of the ground beef.

crabmeat & cream cheese empanadas
Prepare the basic recipe, using 8 ounces crabmeat, 8 ounces softened cream cheese, and 1 tablespoon bottled chipotle sauce in place of the ground beef, garlic, tomato purée, raisins, and olives.

spicy chicken & cheese empanadas
Prepare the basic recipe, using 1 cup cooked and shredded chicken, 8 ounces softened cream cheese, and 1 tablespoon bottled chipotle sauce in place of the ground beef, garlic, tomato purée, raisins, and olives.

banana-rum empanadas
Prepare the basic recipe, using 3 mashed ripe bananas and 1/4 cup dark rum in place of the ground beef, garlic, tomato purée, raisins, and olives.

sun-dried tomato & goat cheese empanadas
Prepare the basic recipe, using 8 ounces softened goat cheese, 1/4 cup chopped sun-dried tomatoes, and 1/4 cup chopped black olives in place of the ground beef, garlic, tomato purée, raisins, and green olives.

soups & salads

Cool and refreshing salads — some with the welcome crunch of jicama — make a hot day more bearable. When the cold nights come, hot and steamy soups with the fragrance of Mexican seasonings warm body and soul.

desert cactus soup

see variations page 73

Thorny pads of prickly pear cactus from desert areas in northern Mexico are despined, cooked, and then cooked with broth for this delicious soup.

1/2 cup chopped onion
1 tbsp. olive oil
1 lb. nopalitos (page 17)

4 cups chicken broth
sour cream, diced tomatoes, and chopped
  cilantro, to garnish

Sauté the onion in olive oil in a large saucepan over medium-high heat. Add the nopalitos and chicken broth. Bring to a boil, then reduce the heat and simmer for 15 minutes. Garnish each bowl with sour cream, diced tomatoes, and cilantro before serving.

Serves 4–6

gazpacho with crèma & fresh cilantro

see variations page 74

Brought from Spain to Mexico, this refreshing cold vegetable soup is perfect in warm weather. Top it with a dollop of Mexican crème fraîche known as crèma (available in many supermarkets) and a sprinkle of fresh cilantro.

2 lbs. fresh ripe tomatoes, chopped and peeled
1 cup peeled and finely chopped seedless cucumber
1 red bell pepper, seeded and diced
1 small red onion, finely chopped
1/2 lb. country-style bread, crust removed, cut into 1/2-inch pieces (about 4 cups)
1/4 cup fresh lime juice

1/4 cup extra-virgin olive oil
1 garlic clove, minced
1/2 tsp. ground cumin
salt and pepper to taste
1 cup crèma or sour cream, to garnish
1/2 cup chopped fresh cilantro, to garnish

Place tomatoes in a large glass bowl. Stir in the cucumber, bell pepper, onion, bread, lime juice, olive oil, garlic, and cumin. Season to taste with salt and pepper. Let stand at room temperature for 1 hour to release the vegetable juices.

Chill for at least 2 hours or up to 1 day. Serve cold in bowls, garnished with crèma, and sprinkled with cilantro.

Serves 8

mexican roasted corn & chile soup

see variations page 75

Roast the corn and chile in the oven first, then simmer them together in this tasty soup.

4 ears fresh corn, shucked and silk removed
1 tbsp. olive oil
1 large Anaheim chile
1 tsp. ground dried ancho chile

3 cups chicken broth
1 cup heavy cream
salt and pepper to taste
freshly chopped cilantro, to garnish

Brush the corn with olive oil. Place the corn and the Anaheim chile on a baking sheet under the broiler, turning once, until the corn kernels and chile are blackened. Place the chile in a plastic bag, close, and let steam for 5 minutes. Remove the skin under cold, running water. Stem, seed, and chop the chile. With a paring knife, scrape the roasted kernels from each ear of corn.

Combine the chile, corn, dried ancho, and chicken broth in a saucepan over medium-high heat. Bring to a boil, then reduce the heat and let simmer for 5 minutes. Stir in the cream, season to taste, and serve garnished with cilantro.

Serves 4–6

wild mushroom & chipotle soup

see variations page 76

Known as *sopa de hongos salvajes*, this dish is made during the autumn months in the sierra or mountainous areas of Oaxaca and Tlaxcala in central Mexico.

1 lb. fresh wild mushrooms, cleaned and sliced
2 cloves garlic, minced
1/2 cup chopped onion
1 tbsp. olive oil

2 canned chipotles in adobo sauce, chopped
6 cups chicken broth
sour cream, diced tomatoes, and chopped
    cilantro, to garnish

Sauté the mushrooms, garlic, and onion in olive oil in a large saucepan over medium-high heat until the mushrooms have wilted and given off their juices. Add the chipotle and chicken broth. Bring to a boil, then reduce the heat and simmer for 15 minutes. Garnish each bowl with sour cream, diced tomatoes, and cilantro.

Serves 4–6

fresh avocado salad with lime & chiles

see variations page 77

Rich and buttery avocados get a complementary lift from fresh lime juice and chiles in this easy-to-assemble salad. To keep the avocados from discoloring, make the salad right before you want to serve it.

2 ripe avocados, peeled, pitted, and sliced
1 tsp. fresh lime zest
2 tbsp. fresh lime juice
1 tsp. piloncillo or brown sugar

1 tbsp. olive oil
ground dried ancho or chipotle chile
salt
fresh Italian parsley sprigs, to garnish

Arrange the avocado slices on a platter. In a small bowl, whisk the lime zest and juice, brown sugar, and olive oil together. Drizzle the dressing over the avocados. Sprinkle with ancho chile and salt to taste. Garnish with Italian parsley. Serve immediately.

Serves 4

jicama salad with fresh mint

see variations page 78

Mellow, pale jicama is a round root vegetable sometimes referred to as the Mexican potato. Unlike the potato, however, jicama is eaten raw and really comes into its own when paired with fresh herbs, chiles, tropical fruits, and citrus. It's a staple in Mexican salads and is very crunchy when chilled.

1 large jicama (about 1 1/2 lbs.)
1 cup diced red bell pepper
1 cup diced yellow bell pepper
1 cup diced green bell pepper
1 cup peeled and diced cucumber

1 large orange, peeled, sliced, and sectioned
1/2 cup chopped fresh mint
1/2 cup fresh lime juice
ground dried ancho or chipotle chile, to taste

Cut the jicama in half. Peel each half, then cut into quarters. Using a box grater or a food processor fitted with the large grater attachment, grate the jicama and place in a large bowl. Stir in the peppers, cucumber, orange, and mint. Drizzle with lime juice and season to taste with dried ancho. Chill until ready to serve.

Serves 4–6

cabbage, radish & cilantro relish

see variations page 79

Crisp, colorful, and delicious, this slaw-like relish goes well with fish tacos, grilled fish fillets, chicken, or pork.

1 cup finely shredded green cabbage
1 cup thinly sliced radishes
1/2 cup finely chopped green onion
2 tbsp. finely chopped fresh cilantro

for the dressing:
3 tbsp. fresh orange juice
2 tbsp. fresh lime juice
2 tbsp. vegetable oil
salt and pepper

In a large bowl, combine the cabbage, radishes, green onion, and cilantro. In a small bowl, whisk the juices and oil together, then season to taste. Pour over the vegetables and toss to blend. Serve immediately.

Serves 4–6

fiesta slaw

see variations page 80

With its fresh lime, chile, and cilantro flavors, this side dish is a wonderful complement to fish tacos, grilled fish and shellfish, chicken, or pork.

for the dressing
1 small red onion, thinly sliced
1 small red chile, minced
grated zest of 1 lime
juice of 2 limes

1 (10-oz.) package finely shredded cabbage or coleslaw mix
1/2 cup chopped fresh cilantro
olive oil for drizzling
salt and pepper

Combine the onion, chile, lime zest, and lime juice in a small bowl, tossing to coat all pieces. Cover and refrigerate until ready to use. When ready to serve, place the cabbage and cilantro in a large serving bowl. Add the onion mixture. Drizzle with olive oil to just moisten, season with salt and pepper, and stir to combine thoroughly. Serve immediately.

Serves 4

grilled shrimp & mango salad with chipotle–lime vinaigrette

see variations page 81

Fresh shrimp and tropical fruit from Baja on the Pacific or the Yucatán Peninsula in the Caribbean make this seaside salad a hit in hot weather.

for the vinaigrette
1 canned chipotle chile in adobo sauce, minced
grated zest of 1 lime
2 tbsp. fresh lime juice
1/2 cup chopped fresh cilantro
1/2 cup olive oil, plus more for brushing

1 lb. peeled and deveined large shrimp
salt and pepper
4 cups fresh salad greens
1 large mango, pitted, peeled, and sliced

For the vinaigrette, combine the chipotle, lime zest and juice, cilantro, and olive oil in a small bowl. Set aside.

Prepare a hot fire in your grill. Brush the shrimp and mango with olive oil, season to taste, and grill on both sides until you have good grill marks and the shrimp are opaque, about 1–2 minutes per side. Arrange the salad greens on plates, top with shrimp and mango, and drizzle with the vinaigrette.

Serves 4

mercado fruit salad with honey-lime dressing

see variations page 82

The walled entrance to the outdoor market in Tepoztlán, near Mexico City, is covered in colorful mosaics with scenes from the ancient Aztecs to Spanish and French colonial days. But what's unique about these mosaics is that they're made with local seeds and beans. On market day, shoppers eat their meals at the mercado, including a fruit salad like this one. Use whatever fruit is in season.

1 cup chopped fresh mango or papaya
1 cup fresh blueberries
1 cup chopped fresh honeydew melon
1 cup fresh pineapple chunks
1 cup seedless red or green grapes

1 tbsp. fresh orange zest
1/2 cup fresh orange juice
1 tbsp. fresh lemon juice
1/3 cup honey
1/4 cup fresh lime juice

Combine the fruits in a large bowl. Stir the orange zest, fresh orange juice, and the lemon juice in a small bowl, then pour over the fruit. Toss gently to blend. Cover and refrigerate until ready to serve. Right before serving, whisk the honey and lime juice together in a small bowl, pour over the salad, and toss to blend. Serve salad in glass dishes.

Serves 4–6

aztec vegetable & amaranth salad bowl

see variations page 83

Amaranth is a small, round grain that was a staple food of the ancient Aztecs. It's available in bulk in the health food aisle and, when cooked, can be used like rice or pasta in salads. Quinoa can be substituted for the amaranth, if you wish. Serve this salad right away so the avocado doesn't discolor.

1 cup raw amaranth (or quinoa)
2 cups fresh or frozen and thawed corn kernels
1 red bell pepper, stemmed, seeded, and sliced
1 cup halved cherry tomatoes
1/2 cup chopped green onions
1 large avocado, pitted, peeled, and sliced
chopped fresh cilantro and pepitas (toasted
    pumpkin seeds), to garnish

for the dressing
1/2 cup olive oil
1 garlic clove, minced
1/4 cup fresh lime juice
1/2 tsp. ground dried ancho chile
salt and pepper to taste

Bring 2 cups of water to a boil in a large saucepan. Add the amaranth and cook, covered, for 15 minutes or until the amaranth is tender. Drain. In a large bowl, combine the cooked amaranth with corn, bell pepper, tomatoes, green onions, and avocado.

In a small bowl, whisk the olive oil, garlic, lime juice, and ancho chile together. Season to taste. Toss the amaranth mixture with the dressing and garnish with cilantro and toasted pumpkin seeds.

Serves 4–6

variations

desert cactus soup

see base recipe page 53

desert cactus soup with chorizo
Prepare the basic recipe, adding 1 pound sliced chorizo to the onion
to brown.

desert cactus soup with avocado
Prepare the basic recipe, garnishing with sliced avocado in addition to the
other garnishes.

desert cactus soup with chicken
Prepare the basic recipe, adding 2 cups cooked, shredded chicken to
the broth.

pantry shelf cactus soup
Prepare the basic recipe, using 1 (14-oz.) can nopalitos, drained, in place of
preparing fresh cactus.

gazpacho with crèma & fresh cilantro

see base recipe page 54

grilled gazpacho

Grill the tomatoes, slices of red onion, and whole red bell pepper over a medium-hot fire until you have good grill marks. Chop the tomatoes and onion. Remove the skin from the bell pepper and chop. Then prepare the basic recipe.

mango & peach gazpacho

Prepare the basic recipe, using 2 cups chopped and peeled mango and 2 cups chopped and peeled peach in place of tomatoes, cucumber, bell pepper, onion, and bread. Add 1 cup mango nectar, 1 cup Chardonnay, and 10 fresh lime leaves cut into fine shreds. Omit the crèma, cilantro, and garlic and garnish with fresh mint sprigs.

cucumber & suero de leche gazpacho

Prepare the basic recipe, using an additional 1 cup chopped seedless cucumber in place of the tomatoes and bell pepper. Stir in 2 cups buttermilk (suero de leche) right before serving.

orange-tomato gazpacho

Prepare the basic recipe, adding 1 cup fresh orange juice and 2 teaspoons finely grated orange zest.

variations

mexican roasted corn & chile soup

see base recipe page 57

mexican roasted tomato soup
Prepare the basic recipe, using chopped tomatoes in place of corn.

grilled onion & chile soup
Prepare the basic recipe, using 2 cups grilled onion in place of corn.

corn & black bean soup
Prepare the basic recipe, using 2 ears of corn instead of 4. Add 1 cup canned black beans with the chicken broth and proceed with the recipe.

roasted corn, chile, & chicken soup
Prepare the basic recipe, adding 2 cups cooked, shredded chicken during the last minutes of simmering.

roasted zucchini & chile soup
Prepare the basic recipe, using chopped zucchini in place of corn.

variations

wild mushroom & chipotle soup

see base recipe page 59

wild mushroom & crèma soup
Prepare the basic recipe, stirring in 1/2 cup crèma or sour cream right
before serving.

wild mushroom & roasted corn soup
Prepare the basic recipe, stirring in 1 cup roasted corn kernels
before simmering.

wild mushroom & toasted cumin soup
Prepare the basic recipe, stirring in 1 teaspoon toasted cumin seed before
simmering. Toast cumin seed by heating it in a dry skillet over high heat
until it smells aromatic, about 1 minute. Remove from the heat and add to
the soup.

wild mushroom & chipotle soup with guacamole topper
Prepare the basic recipe. Serve each bowl with a spoonful of authentic
guacamole (page 30) in the center of the soup and garnish with chopped
cilantro, omitting the sour cream and tomato garnish.

fresh avocado salad with lime & chiles

see base recipe page 61

grilled avocado salad with lime & chiles

Halve and pit the avocados, but do not peel. Grill the avocado halves, cut-side down, on a medium-hot barbecue grill outside or indoors on a grill pan for 2–3 minutes or until you have good grill marks. Slice and peel the avocado and proceed with the basic recipe.

orange & avocado salad with lime & chiles

Prepare the basic recipe, adding 1 large orange, cut into small wedges, to the platter.

tomato & avocado salad with jalapeño dressing

Prepare the basic recipe, adding 1 cup cherry tomatoes to the platter and 1 stemmed, seeded, and finely chopped fresh jalapeño to the dressing.

avocado & grilled shrimp salad with lime & chiles

Prepare the basic recipe, adding 1 pound grilled large shrimp to the platter. To prepare the shrimp, brush the peeled and deveined shrimp with olive oil and season with salt and pepper. Grill the shrimp indoors, turning, on a grill pan for 2–3 minutes per side or until the shrimp have good grill marks and are opaque and cooked through.

jicama salad with fresh mint

see base recipe page 63

jicama salad with fresh orange & cilantro-lime vinaigrette
Prepare the basic recipe, using 1/2 cup chopped fresh cilantro in place of mint.

jicama & watermelon salad
Prepare the basic recipe, using 3 cups finely chopped watermelon in place of the red, green, and yellow bell peppers.

jicama, honeydew & cantaloupe salad
Prepare the basic recipe, using 1 1/2 cups finely chopped honeydew melon and 1 1/2 cups finely chopped cantaloupe in place of the red, green, and yellow bell peppers.

jicama salad with cucumber & lime
Prepare the basic recipe, using 3 additional cups finely chopped cucumber in place of the red, green, and yellow bell peppers.

variations

cabbage, radish & cilantro relish

see base recipe page 64

citrus & herb relish
Prepare the basic recipe, using 1 cup fresh orange segments in place
of radishes.

orange & cilantro relish
Prepare the basic recipe, using 2 cups fresh orange segments in place of the
cabbage and radishes.

mexican corn relish
Prepare the basic recipe, using 1 cup cooked corn kernels and 1 cup diced
red bell pepper in place of the cabbage and radishes.

carrot, onion & jalapeño relish
Prepare the basic recipe, using 1 cup grated carrots and 1 cup stemmed,
seeded, and diced fresh jalapeño in place of the cabbage and radishes.

variations

fiesta slaw

see base recipe page 67

baja slaw
Prepare the basic recipe, using a small green chile in place of the red.

cilantro slaw
Prepare the basic recipe, using 4 chopped green onions in place of the red onion and a small green chile in place of the red.

mexican slaw with chipotle-lime vinaigrette
Prepare the basic recipe, adding 1 canned chipotle chile in adobo sauce, finely chopped, to the dressing.

hot & spicy slaw
Prepare the basic recipe, adding 1 stemmed, seeded, and chopped fresh habañero chile to the slaw.

grilled shrimp & mango salad with chipotle–lime vinaigrette

see base recipe page 69

grilled scallops & mango salad with chipotle–lime vinaigrette
Prepare the basic recipe, using scallops in place of shrimp.

grilled chicken & pineapple salad with chipotle–lime vinaigrette
Prepare the basic recipe, using 1 pound boneless, skinless chicken breast in place of shrimp and fresh pineapple rings in place of mango.
Grill the chicken for 4 or 5 minutes per side or until 165°F in thickest part. Chop the chicken and arrange the pieces on the salad.

grilled swordfish and papaya salad with chipotle–lime vinaigrette
Prepare the basic recipe, using grilled swordfish steaks in place of shrimp and fresh papaya in place of mango. Grill the swordfish for 4–5 minutes per side, then chop and arrange on the salad.

grilled tuna & papaya salad with chipotle–lime vinaigrette
Prepare the basic recipe, using fresh sashimi-grade tuna in place of shrimp and fresh papaya in place of mango. Sear the tuna over a very hot fire, turning once, until you have good grill marks on both sides but the tuna is still raw, then chop and arrange on the salad.

variations

mercado fruit salad with honey-lime dressing

see base recipe page 71

papaya, mango & lime salad with mango cream
Prepare the basic recipe, using a total of 5 cups chopped fresh papaya and mango, in place of the mixed fruits; lime zest and juice in place of orange zest and juice; and mango cream (page 27) in place of honey-lime dressing.

grilled citrus salad with honey-lime dressing
Prepare a hot fire in your grill. Peel and slice 2 grapefruits, 4 oranges, 2 limes, and 2 lemons. Brush the cut sides with vegetable oil. Grill, turning once, until you have good grill marks, about 1-2 minutes per side. Arrange on a platter and drizzle with the honey-lime dressing.

fresh melon salad with honey-lime dressing
Prepare the basic recipe, using 2 cups chopped and seeded fresh watermelon and 3 cups chopped fresh honeydew melon in place of the mixed fruits.

mercado berry salad with honey-lime dressing
Prepare the basic recipe, using 3 cups fresh blueberries and 2 cups fresh hulled and halved strawberries in place of the mixed fruits.

variations

aztec vegetable & amaranth salad bowl

see base recipe page 72

yucatán rainforest platter
Prepare the basic recipe, using 4 cups chopped tropical fruits in place of the corn, bell pepper, cherry tomatoes, and green onions.

tex-mex grilled vegetable platter
Prepare the basic recipe, grilling the red bell pepper, cherry tomatoes, and green onions before adding them to the salad.

mexico city market-day platter
Prepare the basic recipe, adding cooked chorizo to the platter.

sonoran desert platter
Prepare the basic recipe, adding nopalitos (page 17) or canned nopalitos to the platter.

poultry

Poultry has always been a favorite Mexican food.
Usually, poultry is slow-simmered, then picked from
the bone and shredded to use in fillings for burritos,
enchiladas, chilequiles, tamales, tacos, or quesadillas.
But it can also be grilled for fajitas or roasted whole.

oaxacan chicken in mole

see variations page 105

Conquered by the Aztecs in 1482 and by the Spanish in 1522, Oaxaca is a province known for the variety of its moles (sauces made by grinding many ingredients together). Chicken slowly simmered in a spicy mole becomes fall-apart tender as well as uniquely flavored. Serve this dish over rice.

2 large frying chickens, about 3 lbs. each,
    cut up
1 large onion, sliced
4 cloves garlic, chopped
3 cups chicken broth
basic mole (page 17)
chopped fresh cilantro, to garnish

Place the chicken pieces in a large saucepan. Add the onion, garlic, and chicken broth, and bring to a boil. Reduce the heat to simmer. Cook, covered, for 45 minutes or until the chicken is tender and cooked through. Remove the chicken from the broth; set broth aside.

When cool enough to handle, remove skin, fat, and bones from chicken and discard. Cut the chicken meat into large pieces and reserve. Strain the broth, then return it to the pan. Stir in the basic mole and bring to a boil over medium-high heat. Stir in the chicken and heat through. Serve over hot rice, garnished with cilantro.

Serves 6–8

chicken barbacoa

see variations page 106

Barbacoa — foods over an indirect fire outdoors — are popular in Mexico. Cabrito (goat) is the choice in the north, lamb in central Mexico, and pork in the Yucatán, but everyone loves chicken. Mesquite chips provide a regional "kiss of smoke" flavor.

1 cup mesquite wood chips
1 roasting chicken (about 4 lbs.), cleaned, with
    giblets and neck removed
2 tbsp. olive oil
1 1/2 tsp. garlic powder

1 1/2 tsp. black pepper
1 tsp. dried anise or fennel
1 1/2 tsp. ground dried ancho chile
1 tsp. salt, or to taste

Prepare an indirect fire in your grill — the coals or heat to one side and no heat on the other side. For a charcoal grill, soak the mesquite chips in water in a bowl; drain. For a gas grill, place the dry chips in a smoker box or an aluminum foil packet.

Brush the chicken with olive oil. Combine the spices and salt in a small bowl, then sprinkle the chicken all over with the mixture. Place the chicken, breast-side down, on the indirect side, away from the heat. If using a charcoal grill, sprinkle the hot coals with the soaked mesquite chips. For a gas grill, place the smoker box or foil packet as close as possible to the gas flame. When you see the first wisp of smoke, close the grill lid. Cook, covered, for 1 hour, turning the chicken at intervals to brown evenly, until a meat thermometer inserted in the thickest part of the thigh registers 170°F. The meat should not be at all pink. Serve hot.

Serves 4

chilaquiles

see variations page 107

Ideal for a casual meal, this tortilla chicken casserole with green chile sauce is comfort food with a twist. In Tijuana, chilaquiles are a favorite breakfast side dish.

4 cups shredded cooked chicken
salsa verde (page 214)
1 cup Mexican crèma or sour cream
1/2 cup heavy cream

12 (6-inch) fresh corn tortillas, cut into
    1/4-inch-wide strips (store-bought or
    homemade)
4 cups (1 lb.) shredded Mexican cheese, such as
    Monterey Jack or Chihuahua

Preheat the oven to 350°F. Arrange half the chicken in a 9x13-inch pan. Top with half the salsa verde. Mix the crèma or sour cream and heavy cream together and spread half over the salsa. Top with half the tortilla strips and half the shredded cheese. Repeat the process.

Bake for 45 minutes or until browned and bubbling. To serve, let cool slightly, then cut into squares.

Serves 8

chicken enchiladas

see variations page 108

Enchiladas are a Mexican family staple, using common ingredients — prepared salsas, cooked meats, cheese, and corn tortillas. They're great for a casual meal or to feed a crowd.

salsa roja (page 23)
2 cups grated Monterey Jack or Chihuahua
    cheese
3 cups shredded or chopped cooked chicken

salt to taste
vegetable oil for frying
12 (5- to 6-inch) corn tortillas (store-bought or
    homemade)

Preheat the oven to 450°F. In a medium bowl, mix 1/4 cup salsa roja and 1/4 cup cheese with the chicken. Season with salt to taste. Coat the bottom of a medium skillet with oil, and place pan over medium-high heat. When the skillet is hot, dip each tortilla into the remaining salsa to lightly coat, then fry on both sides until softened. Transfer to a plate. Add more oil when necessary.

Spread out the tortillas on a flat surface and place 1/4 cup of the chicken filling in the center of each one. Roll up. Place each roll in a 9x13-inch baking pan. Spoon the remaining sauce over the rolled tortillas and sprinkle with the remaining cheese. Bake for 20 minutes or until heated through and bubbling.

Serves 6–8

tortilla soup

see variations page 109

With this savory soup, you get a fiesta of flavors — and colors — all in one bowl.

1/4 cup vegetable oil
6 (5- to 6-inch) fresh corn tortillas (store-
    bought or homemade), cut in half, then into
    1/4-inch strips
1 cup chopped onion
2 cloves garlic, minced
1 Anaheim, poblano, or large jalapeño chile,
    stemmed, seeded, and chopped
4 cups chicken broth

1 (14 1/2-oz.) can chopped tomatoes, drained
1 1/2 cups shredded cooked chicken
salt and pepper to taste
1 cup shredded Monterey Jack or Chihuahua
    cheese, to garnish
1 ripe avocado, pitted, peeled, and sliced, to
    garnish
1/4 cup chopped fresh cilantro, to garnish

In a large saucepan, heat the oil over medium-high heat. Fry the tortilla strips in batches until crisp and drain on paper towels. Add the onion, garlic, and chile to the remaining oil and cook, stirring, until the onion has softened, about 4 minutes. Stir in the broth, tomatoes, and chicken, and bring to a boil. Reduce the heat and simmer, covered, for 15 minutes to let the flavors blend.

To serve, divide half the fried tortilla strips among 4 bowls. Ladle in the soup, then garnish with shredded cheese, avocado slices, chopped cilantro, and the remaining tortilla strips.

Serves 4

anticuchos de pollo

see variations page 110

These grilled chicken skewers are delicious street food that you might find at a mercado or market, but they're just as delicious from your own backyard grill. For a special touch, use shards of fresh sugarcane, available at Hispanic markets, as skewers.

2 lbs. boneless, skinless chicken breasts cut into
   2-inch pieces
6–8 wooden skewers, soaked in water for
   30 minutes and drained
2 cups mango nectar

1/4 cup spicy barbecue sauce
1 tsp. ground dried chipotle chile
1 tbsp. vegetable oil
freshly chopped cilantro, to garnish

Thread the chicken onto the skewers, being careful not to crowd the pieces. In a bowl, whisk together the mango nectar, barbecue sauce, chipotle, and vegetable oil. Reserve half the mixture and brush the other half over the chicken.

Prepare a medium-hot fire in your grill. Grill the skewers for 3–5 minutes per side, turning once, until done. Serve over Mexican confetti rice (page 210), drizzle with the remaining sauce, and sprinkle with chopped cilantro.

Serves 6–8

chicken tamales with yellow mole

see variations page 111

Also known as mole amarillo, the yellowish-orange sauce that accompanies these tamales is very versatile — it's delicious on just about anything.

1 recipe yellow mole (page 18)
1 1/2 cups instant corn masa flour
1 1/4 cups chicken broth
1 cup shredded cooked chicken

10 dried cornhusks, soaked in water for
    30 minutes and drained

Make the yellow mole, and while it is simmering, make the tortillas. Place the masa flour in a bowl. Stir in the chicken broth to make a soft dough, adding a little more water if necessary. Divide the dough into 10 portions and form each portion into a ball. Place each ball of dough between 2 unopened plastic sandwich bags, then press to a 5- or 6-inch round in a tortilla press.

Place 1 tablespoon of yellow mole and 1 tablespoon of shredded chicken in the middle of each tortilla. Fold in the sides and place in the damp cornhusk. Secure the ends with string so that each tamale is completely enclosed in the husk. Arrange the tamales upright in a steamer, not letting them touch the water, and steam for 30 minutes.

To serve, unwrap each tamale and serve with more yellow mole.

Serves 4–6

huevos rancheros

see variations page 112

Before you can have chicken, you have to start with eggs, right? Ranch-style eggs with soft-fried corn tortillas are a popular dish at many Mexican eateries, from cafés to cantinas. Customize this dish with your choice of garnish.

2 tbsp. vegetable oil
6 fresh corn or flour tortillas (store-bought or
    homemade, page 15, 16)
6 large eggs

sliced avocado, fresh cilantro sprigs, chopped
    green onions, shredded cheese, and lime
    wedges, to garnish
1 recipe salsa cruda (page 21)

Heat the oil over medium-high heat in a large skillet. When the oil is hot, fry the corn tortillas for about 10 seconds on each side. Drain on paper towels. Crack the eggs into the hot oil and fry the eggs to your desired doneness. To serve, place a soft tortilla on each plate and top with an egg and your chosen garnishes. Serve the salsa on the side.

Serves 3–6

mesquite-grilled turkey piñon

see variations page 113

Pair the turkey with this salsa made from piñon nuts — from pine trees in northern Mexico.

for the salsa
3/4 cup toasted pine nuts
3 hard-cooked large egg yolks
2 tbsp. capers, drained
2 tbsp. caper juice
1 cup half-and-half or light cream
salt and pepper to taste

1 cup mesquite wood chips
4 (6-oz.) turkey breast tenderloin steaks
olive oil for brushing

To make the salsa, in a blender or food processor, combine the pine nuts, egg yolks, capers, caper juice, and half-and-half. Blend until smooth. Season with salt and pepper to taste and set aside.

Prepare a medium-hot fire in your grill. For a charcoal grill, soak the mesquite chips in water in a bowl; drain. For a gas grill, place dry wood chips in a smoker box or an aluminum foil packet. Brush the turkey tenderloins with olive oil, and season with salt and pepper to taste. If using a charcoal grill, sprinkle the hot coals with the soaked mesquite chips. For a gas grill, place the smoker box or foil packet as close as possible to the gas flame. When you see the first wisp of smoke, place the turkey on the grill and close the grill lid. Cook, covered, for 6 minutes; turn, cover, and grill another 7 minutes or until a meat thermometer inserted in the thickest part registers 170°F. Serve hot with the salsa.

Serves 4

quail with rose petals

see variations page 114

Laura Esquivel made this hauntingly delicious dish popular in her novel *Like Water for Chocolate*. Use organic or unsprayed red rosebuds, the most fragrant you can find.

4 quail, cleaned, rinsed, and patted dry

for the marinade
6 red rosebuds, organic or unsprayed
1/2 cup sliced almonds
2 garlic cloves

2 tbsp. unsalted butter
2 tbsp. honey
2 tbsp. cornmeal
2 tbsp. anise or fennel seed
salt and pepper to taste

Preheat the oven to 400°F.

Tear the petals from the rosebuds and place them in a food processor or blender along with the almonds and garlic. Run on pulse to finely chop. In a saucepan over medium heat, melt the butter and honey together. Add the rose mixture, cornmeal, and anise or fennel seed, and stir until well blended and fragrant. Season to taste.

Place the quail on a baking sheet and brush with half of the mixture. Roast for 20 minutes, baste with the remaining rose mixture, and continue roasting until a meat thermometer inserted in the thickest part of the thigh registers 170°F. The meat should not be at all pink.

Serves 4

soft tacos with duck

see variations page 115

Mexico is part of the fly-over zone for wildfowl of all kinds going south for the winter.
You won't find soft tacos with duck on fast-food menus, but you will in hunters' homes.

4 Long Island duck breasts, boned
2 tbsp. honey
1 clove garlic, minced
1 tbsp. fresh lime juice
salt and pepper to taste
8 large flour tortillas, warmed

1 recipe pineapple, mango, or papaya salsa
  (page 20, 21)
fresh chopped cilantro

With a sharp knife, score the fat side of the duck breasts in a cross-hatch pattern. Heat a
large skillet over medium-high heat. Cook the duck breasts, fat-side down, for 3–4 minutes
or until the fat has browned.

In a small bowl, combine the honey, garlic, and lime juice. Turn the duck and brush or drizzle
with half of this mixture; reserve the rest. Cook the duck until medium-rare, about 3 more
minutes. Remove from the heat, season to taste, and let rest for 5 minutes.

Slice the duck on the diagonal. Place the slices in the center of each warmed flour tortilla,
drizzle with the remaining honey mixture, top with salsa and cilantro, roll up and serve.

Serves 8

variations

oaxacan chicken in mole

see base recipe page 85

turkey in mole
Prepare the basic recipe, using 1 small turkey (about 6 pounds), cut up,
or 2 turkey breasts, in place of chicken.

turkey in green mole
Prepare the basic recipe, using 1 small turkey (about 6 pounds), cut up,
or 2 turkey breasts, in place of chicken, and green mole (page 19) in place of
basic mole.

duck in mole
Prepare the basic recipe, using 1 large (about 5 pounds) Long Island duckling,
cut up, in place of chicken.

variations

chicken barbacoa

see base recipe page 86

turkey breast barbacoa
Prepare the basic recipe, using a turkey breast in place of the
roasting chicken.

duck breast barbacoa
Prepare the basic recipe, using 4 Long Island duckling breasts in place
of the roasting chicken.

chicken wings barbacoa
Prepare the basic recipe, using 4 pounds chicken wings in place of the
roasting chicken.

beef barbacoa
Prepare the basic recipe, using a 3 1/2-pound boneless beef chuck roast in
place of the roasting chicken and oregano in place of the anise or fennel.

chilaquiles

see base recipe page 88

turkey chilaquiles
Prepare the basic recipe, using shredded cooked turkey in place of chicken.

duck chilaquiles
Prepare the basic recipe, using shredded cooked duck in place of chicken.

shrimp chilaquiles
Prepare the basic recipe, using cooked large shrimp in place of chicken.

chicken enchiladas

see base recipe page 90

vegetarian cheese & chile enchiladas
Prepare the basic recipe, using salsa verde (page 214) in place of salsa roja
and 3 more cups grated Monterey Jack cheese combined with 1/4 cup canned
chopped green chiles in place of chicken.

shrimp enchiladas
Prepare the basic recipe, using 3 cups cooked shrimp in place of chicken.

beef enchiladas
Prepare the basic recipe, using 3 cups shredded cooked beef in place
of chicken.

variations

tortilla soup

see base recipe page 93

vegetarian tortilla soup
Prepare the basic recipe, using vegetable broth in place of chicken broth and black beans in place of shredded chicken.

tortilla soup with grilled shrimp
Prepare the basic recipe, using grilled shrimp in place of shredded chicken.

tortilla soup with turkey
Prepare the basic recipe, using shredded cooked turkey in place of chicken.

variations

anticuchos de pollo

see base recipe page 95

grilled pork skewers
Prepare the basic recipe, using pork tenderloin in place of chicken.

grilled fish skewers
Prepare the basic recipe, using halibut, monkfish, or salmon in place of chicken.

grilled beef skewers
Prepare the basic recipe, using beef sirloin in place of chicken.

grilled shrimp skewers
Prepare the basic recipe, using large, raw, peeled and deveined shrimp in place of chicken.

chicken tamales with yellow mole

see base recipe page 96

chicken tamales with green mole
Prepare the basic recipe, using green mole (page 19) in place of yellow mole.

chicken tamales with salsa roja
Prepare the basic recipe, using salsa roja (page 23) in place of the mole sauce.

chicken tamales with tomatillo salsa
Prepare the basic recipe, using pantry shelf tomatillo salsa (page 20) in place of yellow mole.

huevos rancheros

see base recipe page 98

huevos con queso
Prepare the basic recipe, sprinkling the eggs with cheese as they are frying.

huevos con cebolla
After frying the corn tortillas, fry 1 finely chopped onion in the oil for about 5 minutes or until soft. Crack the eggs over the onion and continue with the basic recipe.

chorizo ranchero
Prepare the basic recipe, replacing the eggs with slices of fried chorizo.

huevos cilantro
Prepare the basic recipe and serve with cilantro salsa (page 26) in place of salsa cruda.

mesquite-grilled turkey piñon

see base recipe page 101

mesquite-grilled chicken piñon
Prepare the basic recipe, using boneless, skinless chicken breasts in place of turkey.

mesquite-grilled lamb piñon
Prepare the basic recipe, using 4 lamb steaks in place of turkey, but grill them only 3 minutes per side.

mesquite-grilled salmon piñon
Prepare the basic recipe, using a 2-pound salmon fillet in place of turkey, but grill it only 5 minutes per side.

mesquite-grilled pork piñon
Prepare the basic recipe, using 4 pork chops in place of turkey.

variations

quail with rose petals

see base recipe page 102

cornish game hens with rose petals
Prepare the basic recipe, using Cornish game hens in place of the quail.

chicken breasts with rose petals
Prepare the basic recipe, using bone-in chicken breasts in place of the quail.

duck legs with rose petals
Prepare the basic recipe, using 8 Long Island duck legs in place of the quail.

variations

soft tacos with duck

see base recipe page 104

soft tacos with chicken
Prepare the basic recipe, using chicken breasts in place of duck. Do not score.
Cook in 2 tablespoons vegetable oil on both sides, brushing the cooked side
with the honey mixture, until done.

soft tacos with turkey
Prepare the basic recipe, using 4 turkey breast slices in place of duck.
Do not score. Sauté in 2 tablespoons vegetable oil on both sides, brushing
the cooked side with the honey mixture, until done.

soft tacos with pheasant
Prepare the basic recipe, using 4 pheasant breasts in place of duck.
Do not score. Sauté in 2 tablespoons vegetable oil on both sides, brushing
the cooked side with the honey mixture, until done.

nachos with duck
Prepare the basic recipe. Instead of serving on soft tortillas, cut the cooked
duck breast into small pieces and serve on an ovenproof platter of fried
tortilla crisps. Add chopped fresh papaya, mango, or peach to taste.
Sprinkle with shredded Monterey Jack cheese. Place in a 350°F oven until
the cheese melts, then sprinkle with chopped cilantro and serve hot.

beef

After beef cattle came to Mexico with the Spanish,

large ranches bordering Arizona, New Mexico,

and Texas gave rise to a specific cuisine known as

Tex-Mex, which is centered on beef (simmered and

shredded or grilled), flour tortillas, beans, and chiles.

oak-grilled tri-tip

see variations page 133

Tri-tip is the triangular-shaped roast from the bottom sirloin. To grill it Mexican-style, simply season it with salt and pepper, mop it with Mexican beer, and turn it every 10 minutes until medium-rare. It tastes best on a charcoal grill and is delicious served with warm flour tortillas and frijoles refrito (page 209).

1 tri-tip roast (about 3 lbs.)
salt and pepper to taste
1 cup oak chips or chunks, soaked in water for
    at least 30 minutes and drained
1 cup Mexican beer

Prepare a medium-hot fire in a charcoal grill. Season the roast all over with salt and pepper. Pour the beer in a bowl. Place the drained oak chips on the hot coals. When you see the first wisp of smoke from the wood, place the beef on the grill. Grill the roast, covered, for about 10 minutes on each side, basting with the beer every 5 minutes. The roast is done when the internal temperature reaches 140°F. Let the beef rest for 10 minutes, then slice and serve.

Serves 8–10

sizzling skirt steak fajitas

see variations page 134

Either skirt or flank steak makes incredible fajitas. The trick is to marinate the steak first, cook it only until medium-rare, then slice thinly on the diagonal. Serve your fajitas with store-bought or homemade flour tortillas, guacamole, and pico de gallo.

1/2 cup Mexican beer
2 tbsp. fresh lime juice
1 clove garlic, minced
2 tsp. ground cumin
1 1/2 lbs. skirt steak or flank steak
1 large onion, sliced into 1-inch rounds

1 red bell pepper, stemmed, seeded, and
    quartered
vegetable oil for brushing
salt and pepper to taste

In a sealable plastic bag, combine the beer, lime juice, garlic, and cumin. Add the steak, seal the bag, and toss to cover the meat. Marinate in the refrigerator for at least 1 hour or up to 8 hours.

Prepare a hot fire in your grill or heat a cast-iron fajita pan on the stovetop until very hot. Remove the steak from the marinade, pat it dry, and discard the marinade. Brush the onion slices, red bell pepper, and steak with vegetable oil. Season to taste. Grill the onion and bell pepper for 5-7 minutes per side or until charred and softened. Grill the steak for 2 1/2-3 minutes per side for medium-rare. Let the steak rest for 5 minutes, then slice on the diagonal and serve with the grilled vegetables.

Serves 4

slow-braised mexican short ribs in chipotle sauce

see variations page 135

The longer and slower you braise these ribs, the more tender and flavorful they become. Serve with warm flour tortillas and guacamole or green mole (page 16, 30, 19).

4 lbs. beef short ribs
salt and pepper to taste
2 tbsp. vegetable oil
1 large onion, diced

4 cloves garlic, minced
1 (12-oz.) bottle Mexican beer
2 canned chipotles in adobo sauce, chopped

Season the ribs on both sides. Heat the oil in a heavy, large pot over medium-high heat. Brown the ribs on both sides, in batches, about 15 minutes. Transfer the ribs to a plate.

Cook the onion and garlic in the same pot until the onion is translucent, about 5 minutes. Return the ribs to the pot and add the beer and chipotles. Bring to a boil, then reduce the heat. Simmer, covered, until the ribs are tender, about 3 hours.

Serves 4

carne asada in agua negra marinade

see variations page 136

Carne asada is usually a thin beef steak, either cooked on a comal (griddle) indoors or on a barbecue grill outside. Marinated in a dark mixture of tropical juices, soy sauce, and garlic, this steak can be sliced and served as an entrée or used as a filling for burritos and tacos.

1/3 cup pineapple juice
2 tbsp. fresh lime juice
1/3 cup soy sauce
1 clove garlic, minced
2 tsp. ground cumin

1 1/2 lbs. flank steak
vegetable oil for brushing
salt and pepper to taste
authentic guacamole (page 30), to garnish
pico de gallo (page 15), to garnish

In a sealable plastic bag, combine the juices, soy sauce, garlic, and cumin. Add the steak, seal the bag, and toss to cover the meat. Marinate in the refrigerator for at least 1 hour or up to 8 hours.

Prepare a hot fire in your grill. Remove the steak from the marinade, pat it dry, and discard the marinade. Brush the steak with vegetable oil and season to taste. Grill for 2 1/2–3 minutes per side for medium-rare. Let the steak rest for 5 minutes, then slice on the diagonal and serve with guacamole and pico de gallo.

Serves 4

mexican beef brisket stew

see variations page 137

Known as caldillo (little soup), this brothy stew makes great cold weather fare.

2 tbsp. vegetable oil
2 lbs. beef brisket, diced
1 onion, sliced
3 potatoes, peeled and diced
1 cup chopped canned tomatoes, with liquid

3 jalapeño peppers, stemmed, seeded,
   and minced
3 cloves garlic, minced
1 tsp. salt
2 cups beef broth

Heat the oil over medium-high heat in a heavy, large pot. Brown the beef and onion for about 10 minutes. Add the potatoes, tomatoes, chiles, garlic, salt, and broth. Bring to a boil, then reduce the heat and simmer, covered, for 1–1 1/2 hours or until the beef is tender.

Serves 6–8

grilled steak in salsa roja

see variations page 138

For bold flavor, this steak with its zesty sauce and melted cheese is a winner. Serve with frijoles refritos (page 209) and Mexican confetti rice (page 210).

4 boneless sirloin or rib eye steaks, cut
   1 inch thick
vegetable oil for brushing

salt and pepper to taste
salsa roja (page 23)
1 cup shredded Monterey Jack cheese

Prepare a hot fire in your grill. Brush the steak with vegetable oil and season to taste. Grill for 2 1/2 minutes on one side. Turn, spoon 1 tablespoon salsa roja on each steak, and top each steak with 1/4 cup of cheese. Close the lid of the grill and grill for 2 1/2 minutes more or until the cheese has melted and the steak is medium-rare.

Serves 4

mexican pot roast

see variations page 139

Beef chuck, slow-simmered to a tender turn, is made all the more delicious with
south-of-the-border seasonings.

2 tbsp. vegetable oil
3 lbs. boneless chuck roast
salt and pepper
1 tsp. ground cumin
1 large onion, sliced

2 cloves garlic, minced
1 (14 1/2-oz.) can tomatoes with green chiles,
     with liquid
1 cup bottled chipotle mojo marinade

Heat the oil over medium-high heat in a large pot. Season the beef on both sides with salt,
pepper, and cumin. Brown the beef all over for about 10 minutes. Add the onions, garlic,
tomatoes, and chipotle mojo marinade. Bring to a boil, then reduce the heat and simmer,
covered, for 2–2 1/2 hours or until the beef is tender.

Serves 6-8

chile colorado

see variations page 140

This recipe is the ancestor of chili con carne. The beef is slow-simmered in a red chile broth. Serve it with warm flour tortillas to soak it all up.

for the chile purée

8 dried red chiles, such as guajillo or New
   Mexico
1 cup hot water
2 cloves garlic
1 tsp. ground cumin
1 tsp. dried epazote or oregano leaves
1 (14 1/2-oz.) can chopped tomatoes, with liquid

2 tbsp. vegetable oil
3 lbs. boneless chuck roast, cut into 1-inch
   cubes
salt and pepper
1 large onion, sliced
shredded Monterey Jack cheese, to garnish
pico de gallo (page 15), to garnish
warm flour tortillas, for serving

On a comal (griddle) over medium-high heat, toast the chiles for 2 minutes on each side. Place the toasted chiles in a bowl and pour the hot water over them. Let the chiles soften for 30 minutes, then stem and seed them, reserving the soaking water. Place the chiles, garlic, cumin, epazote, tomatoes, and 1/4 cup of the soaking water in a food processor or blender. Purée until smooth. Set aside.

Heat the oil over medium-high heat in a heavy, large pot. Season the beef and then brown all over for about 20 minutes. Add the sliced onion and chile purée. Bring to a boil, then reduce the heat and simmer, covered, for 2–2 1/2 hours or until the beef is tender. Serve in bowls, topped with shredded Monterey Jack cheese and pico de gallo, and accompanied by flour tortillas.

Serves 6-8

soft beef tacos with salsa

see variations page 141

Tacos have gone so mainstream that many families have a regular "taco night." Fresh, homemade tortillas make all the difference, as do fresh fillings and accompaniments.

1 lb. ground beef
1 cup chopped onion
2 cloves garlic, minced
2 tbsp. taco seasoning
1/2 cup bottled chipotle mojo marinade
1 recipe homemade flour tortillas (page 16) or
    soft corn tortillas (page 15), warmed

salsa cruda (page 21)
sour cream, shredded lettuce, and shredded
    Mexican-blend or Monterey Jack cheese, to
    garnish

In a skillet over medium-high heat, brown the ground beef, onion, and garlic together. Add the taco seasoning and chipotle mojo marinade. Let simmer for 5 minutes.

To serve, place a spoonful of taco meat in the center of each tortilla. Top with salsa and the accompaniments of your choice, and roll up.

Serves 4

variations

oak-grilled tri-tip

see base recipe page 117

oak-grilled tri-tip sandwiches
Prepare the basic recipe and slice the steak. Serve it between two slices of
grilled bread slathered with your favorite salsa or barbecue sauce.

oak-grilled tri-tip fajitas
Prepare the basic recipe, slice the steak, and then cut it into thin strips.
Serve the strips wrapped in a warm flour tortilla with your favorite
condiments.

oak-grilled tri-tip salad
Prepare the basic recipe, slice the steak, and then cut it into thin strips.
Arrange the strips on top of sliced tomatoes. Top with guacamole and
chopped green onions, then serve.

variations

sizzling skirt steak fajitas

see base recipe page 118

sizzling chicken fajitas

Prepare the basic recipe, using boneless, skinless chicken breast in place of steak. Grill for 4–5 minutes per side, turning once, or until done.

sizzling veggie fajitas

Prepare the basic recipe, using portabello mushrooms in place of steak. Marinate for 1 hour, then grill for 2–3 minutes per side or until you have good grill marks.

sizzling lamb fajitas

Prepare the basic recipe, using boneless lamb shoulder in place of steak.

slow-braised mexican short ribs in chipotle sauce

see base recipe page 121

slow-braised mexican short ribs in smoked tomato & chile sauce
Prepare the basic recipe, adding 1 (14 1/2-oz) can chopped tomatoes with liquid and 1 teaspoon liquid smoke flavoring when you add the beer and chipotles to the pot.

slow-braised lamb ribs in chipotle sauce
Prepare the basic recipe, using lamb ribs in place of beef.

slow-braised pork chops in chipotle sauce
Prepare the basic recipe, using pork chops in place of beef short ribs. Bake for 1 hour, covered, or until the pork chops are tender.

variations

carne asada in agua negra marinade

see base recipe page 122

carne asada in mexican beer marinade
Prepare the basic recipe, using Mexican beer in place of soy sauce in the marinade.

carne asada in lime chipotle marinade
Prepare the basic recipe, using bottled chipotle mojo marinade in place of soy sauce in the marinade.

carne asada in margarita marinade
Prepare the basic recipe, using bottled margarita mix in place of soy sauce in the marinade.

carne asada in pineapple-papaya marinade
Prepare the basic recipe, using papaya nectar in place of soy sauce in the marinade.

mexican beef brisket stew

see base recipe page 125

mexican lamb & tomatillo stew
Prepare the basic recipe, using boneless lamb shoulder in place of beef and husked tomatillos in place of tomatoes.

mexican pork & sweet potato stew
Prepare the basic recipe, using boneless pork shoulder in place of beef and sweet potatoes in place of white potatoes.

mexican cabrito stew
Prepare the basic recipe, using boneless cabrito shoulder in place of beef. Shred the meat and serve with warm flour tortillas.

mexican game stew
Prepare the basic recipe, using boneless venison roast in place of beef. Shred the meat and serve with warm flour tortillas.

variations

grilled steak in salsa roja

see base recipe page 127

grilled steak in green mole
Prepare the basic recipe, using green mole (page 19) in place of salsa roja.

grilled steak in chipotle sauce
Prepare the basic recipe, using store-bought chipotle sauce in place of
salsa roja.

grilled steak with cheese & chiles
Prepare the basic recipe, using roasted, chopped poblano chiles on top of the
steak instead of the salsa. Top the chiles with the cheese and serve with your
favorite salsa on the side.

grilled steak with pumpkin seed salsa
Prepare the basic recipe, replacing the salsa roja with pumpkin seed salsa
(page 25).

variations

mexican pot roast

see base recipe page 128

mexican pot roast in a banana leaf
Prepare the basic recipe, omitting the chipotle mojo marinade. Transfer the pot roast and vegetables to the center of a frozen and thawed banana leaf. Wrap the leaf around the pot roast, place in a pan with the seam down, and cook in a 300°F oven for 2 1/2–3 hours or until the beef is tender.

mexican beer-braised pot roast
Prepare the basic recipe, using 1 (12-oz.) bottle Mexican beer in place of chipotle mojo marinade.

mexican smoked tomato & chile pot roast
Prepare the basic recipe, adding 1 teaspoon liquid smoke flavoring and 1 stemmed, seeded, and chopped fresh jalapeño chile.

chipotle pot roast
Prepare the basic recipe, adding 3 canned and chopped chipotles in adobo, with some of the adobo sauce.

chile colorado

see base recipe page 131

turkey chile colorado
Prepare the basic recipe, using boneless, skinless turkey in place of the beef.

chicken chile colorado
Prepare the basic recipe, using boneless, skinless chicken in place of the beef.

vegetarian chile colorado
Prepare the basic recipe, using 2 pounds texturized vegetable protein (TVP) or firm tofu in place of the beef. Simmer for 1 hour or until the flavors blend.

chile con carne
Prepare the basic recipe, using 2 pounds ground beef in place of the cubed beef and adding 1 (14 1/2-oz.) can chili beans. Simmer for 1 hour or until the flavors blend.

variations

soft beef tacos with salsa

see base recipe page 132

soft chicken tacos with salsa
Prepare the basic recipe, using ground or finely chopped chicken in place of beef.

soft pork tacos with salsa
Prepare the basic recipe, using ground pork in place of beef.

soft seafood tacos with salsa
Prepare the basic recipe, using raw, peeled, and deveined shrimp in place of beef.

soft grilled vegetable tacos with salsa
Prepare the basic recipe, using 2 cups sliced onions, zucchini, and yellow summer squash in place of beef. Brush the slices with olive oil and grill on both sides until you have good grill marks. Season to taste.

pork & lamb

Although the Maya and Aztecs hunted wild pigs known as peccaries, domestic pigs and sheep came to Mexico from Spain. Simmered with Mexican seasonings, wrapped in banana leaves and roasted or grilled, pork and lamb have become integral parts of the cuisine.

pork carnitas

see variations page 160

Shredded carnitas or "little meats," slowly braised in a flavorful broth, are delicious in tacos, burritos, tamales, and other dishes.

5 lbs. boneless pork shoulder or butt
4 cups chicken broth
1 large onion, quartered
1 tbsp. coriander seeds
1 tbsp. cumin seeds

1 tsp. dried epazote or oregano leaves
3 canned chipotles in adobo sauce
2 bay leaves

Place the pork in a large saucepan over medium-high heat and brown the meat on both sides. Add the broth, onion, seeds, epazote, chipotles, and bay leaves, and bring to a boil. Reduce heat and simmer, covered, until tender and meat pulls apart from the bone (about 3 hours).

Remove the meat from the pan and let cool. Strain, then chill the broth. When the meat is cool enough to handle, remove and discard the fat and any gristle. Skim the fat from the broth. Shred the meat and moisten with a little broth. Serve with rice and beans or as a filling in tacos, burritos, tamales, or tostadas.

Serves 8

mayan-style roast
pork in banana leaves

see variations page 161

Although the authentic Mayan recipe involved a wild pig known as a peccary, you can approximate the flavor with domestic pork shoulder. Wrapping the meat in a banana leaf keeps the juices in and adds a slightly herbaceous flavor. In place of banana leaves, you can use a paper bag — just put the meat in the bag and fold the open end closed.

2 tbsp. salt
2 tbsp. pepper
2 tbsp. granulated garlic
2 tbsp. ground dried chipotle pepper

1 (3- to 4-lb.) boneless pork shoulder or butt
frozen banana leaves, thawed
8 oz. queso fresco, crumbled, to garnish
chopped fresh cilantro, to garnish

Prepare an indirect fire in your grill (the coals or heat to one side and no heat on the other side). Combine the salt, pepper, granulated garlic, and dried chipotle. Rub this mixture into the surface of the meat. Place the pork butt on the indirect side of the grill, cover, and cook for 3 hours. Remove. Place pork in the center of a thawed banana leaf section. Wrap the pork and put it in a roasting pan, seam-side down. Cook in a 250°F oven for 2 1/2–3 hours or until tender.

To serve, unwrap the meat and shred it, removing fat and gristle. Serve, garnished with queso fresco and chopped cilantro.

Serves 6–8

chorizo with eggs & potatoes

see variations page 162

Known as *chorizo con huevos y papas*, this breakfast dish is a favorite at many mom-and-pop eateries. Made with shredded or finely chopped pork seasoned with smoked, dried chiles, chorizo has a reddish color and a spicy flavor. The golden raisins add a touch of sweetness to counter the spicy chorizo.

2 tbsp. vegetable oil
1 cup chopped onions
2 large baking potatoes, peeled and finely
    chopped
1/2 lb. chorizo sausage, link (casings removed) or
    bulk-style

3 tbsp. golden raisins, soaked in hot water for
    30 minutes
8 large eggs
chopped fresh cilantro, to garnish
warm corn tortillas, for serving

In a large skillet, heat the vegetable oil over medium-high heat. Add the onions and potatoes and fry, stirring, for 10 minutes. Add the chorizo and cook, stirring to break up the sausage, until the onions and potatoes begin to turn brown. Stir in the raisins. Crack the eggs into the pan, one at a time, and cook them on top of the sausage and vegetables, until the eggs are done. Garnish with chopped cilantro. Serve with warm corn tortillas.

Serves 4

costillar asado

see variations page 163

Seasoned with oregano and garlic, slathered with salsa roja, grilled until tender, then finished with a sweet touch of honey, these succulent ribs are delicious washed down with Mexican beer.

2 tbsp. salt
2 tbsp. pepper
2 tbsp. granulated garlic
2 tbsp. dried oregano

2 racks baby back ribs
1 recipe salsa roja (page 23)
1/2 cup honey

Prepare a medium-hot fire in your grill. Combine the salt, pepper, garlic, and oregano. Season the ribs all over with this mixture. Brush the ribs with half the salsa roja. Grill, turning often, until the meat begins to pull back from the ends of the bone, about 45 minutes. Drizzle the honey over the ribs and continue to grill, turning often, for 15 more minutes. Serve with the remaining salsa roja.

Serves 8

pork & green chile pozole

see variations page 164

Pozole, a stewlike dish made with hominy and pork, is special occasion fare in Mexico. It's especially loved in Guerrero State on the southern Pacific Coast, where restaurants called pozolerias offer their signature versions. Pozole is considered a good cure for hangovers and is often eaten in the early hours after a night on the town.

1 1/2–2 lbs. boneless pork shoulder or butt
2 cups canned white or yellow hominy, drained
4 cloves garlic, minced
6 cups chicken broth
1 cup toasted, shelled pumpkin seeds (pepitas)

1 (13-oz.) can tomatillos, with liquid
1 jalapeño pepper, stemmed and seeded
1/2 cup chopped fresh cilantro
fresh avocado slices and lime wedges, to garnish

Place the pork, hominy, garlic, and broth in a large pot over medium-high heat. Bring to a boil, then simmer, covered, for 1 1/2–2 hours or until the pork is tender. Transfer the pork to a plate and let cool slightly. Let broth cool in the pot.

In a blender or food processor, process the pumpkin seeds until fine, then add the tomatillos, jalapeño, and cilantro. Process until smooth, then set aside.

Shred the pork, removing any fat and gristle. Skim off any fat from the broth and return the meat to the pot. Bring the pozole to a boil again, then reduce the heat. Stir the pepita mixture into the pozole and simmer for 30 minutes. Serve hot in bowls, garnished with avocado slices and lime wedges.

Serves 4–6

pork & poblano tamales

see variations page 165

Because tamales are easy but labor-intensive, they're usually made when families have gathered for holidays or special occasions. They're also made for fundraisers in Mexican communities.

8 oz. lard or vegetable shortening
2 1/2 cups instant corn masa flour
1 tsp. salt
2–2 1/2 cups hot chicken broth
24 dried cornhusks, soaked for 30 minutes in boiling water, drained

for the filling
5 poblano chiles, roasted, stemmed, seeded, and diced
2 cups cooked, shredded pork carnitas (page 143) or pork shoulder
1/2 cup finely chopped fresh cilantro

To make the dough for the tamales, beat the lard in a large bowl with an electric mixer until light and fluffy, about 3 minutes. Place the instant corn masa flour and salt in another large bowl, pour the hot broth over, and stir until you have a soft dough. Beat the masa dough into the lard, a little at a time, until the dough is light and airy.

For the filling, combine the poblanos, pork, and cilantro in a medium bowl.

Arrange the cornhusks on a flat surface. Spread about 1/4 cup of the dough onto the bottom half of each tamal. Place about 1 tablespoon of the filling on the dough. Fold the sides in, then the ends, to enclose the filling. Place the tamales vertically in a steamer; do not let them touch the water. Steam for 45-60 minutes or until the husks pull away from the filling. Serve.

Serves 12

pork chops in green mole

see variations page 166

The natural sweetness of pork gets a kiss of smoke from the grill and a tangy green finishing sauce from the Puebla region in south-central Mexico. A medium fire in your grill will give your pork chops good grill marks and a delicious juicy flavor.

4 boneless pork chops, cut 1-inch thick
1 recipe green mole (page 19)
vegetable oil for brushing

salt and pepper
crèma or sour cream and cilantro sprigs, to
    garnish

In a sealable plastic bag, place the pork chops and half the mole. Seal the bag and toss to cover the meat. Marinate in the refrigerator for at least 1 hour or up to 8 hours.

Prepare a medium fire in your grill. Remove the chops from the marinade, pat them dry, and discard the marinade. Brush the chops with vegetable oil and season to taste. Grill for 10 minutes per side, turning once. Serve each chop with the remaining mole, a dollop of crèma, and a sprig of cilantro.

Serves 4

guava-glazed leg of lamb

see variations page 167

The state of Michoacan on the Pacific coast is noted for its guavas—sweet and aromatic tropical fruits that originated in southern Mexico.

1 1/2 cups guava jelly
4 cloves garlic, minced
2 tbsp. fresh lime juice

1/4 cup tequila
1 leg of lamb (about 3-4 lbs.), boned and tied

For the glaze, whisk the guava jelly and garlic together in a saucepan over medium heat until the jelly has melted and the flavors have blended. Remove from the heat and stir in the lime juice and tequila.

Prepare an indirect fire in your grill—the coals or heat to one side and no heat on the other side. Brush the lamb with half the glaze. Place the lamb on the indirect side, cover, and cook for 1 hour. Turn the lamb over and baste with the remaining glaze. Cover and continue to cook until a meat thermometer in the thickest part reads 135-140°F for medium-rare. To serve, let the lamb rest for 10 minutes, then carve into slices.

Serves 6–8

braised lamb shanks with tequila & chiles

see variations page 168

Braise the lamb shanks in their south-of-the-border broth until meltingly tender, then enjoy them with Mexican confetti rice (page 210) and slow-simmered black beans (page 208).

2 tbsp. vegetable oil
4 lamb shanks
1 cup chopped onion
2 cloves garlic, minced
1 cup chopped, canned tomatoes, drained
2 canned chipotles in adobo sauce, diced, with
    some of the adobo sauce

1/2 cup brewed coffee
2 tbsp. crumbled piloncillo or packed brown
    sugar
1/2 cup tequila
salt and pepper
fresh cilantro sprigs, to garnish

Heat the oil in a large pot over medium-high heat. Add the lamb shanks and brown on all sides, for about 10 minutes. Transfer the shanks to a plate and sauté the onion and garlic for about 4 minutes, or until transparent. Add the tomatoes, chiles, coffee, piloncillo, and tequila, and cook, stirring, until the sugar melts. Return the lamb shanks to the pot and bring to a boil. Reduce the heat and simmer, covered, until the lamb is fork-tender, about 2 1/2–3 hours. Season to taste. Serve with the sauce, garnishing each plate with cilantro sprigs.

Serves 4

veracruz-style grilled leg of lamb

see variations page 169

Veracruz is known for its sugarcane, citrus and tropical fruits, avocados, coffee, and vanilla. Foods cooked in the Veracruz style usually include fresh citrus, and this lamb is a delicious example. Achiote is a packaged seasoning and food dye made from annatto seeds; it is available in the Hispanic section of the grocery store.

for the seasoning
2 tbsp. prepared achiote
1 tsp. black pepper
1 tsp. salt
1 tbsp. freshly grated orange zest
3 tbsp. fresh orange juice
2 tbsp. vegetable oil

1 boned and butterflied leg of lamb,
    about 3-4 lbs.
warm flour tortillas (store-bought or homemade
    page 16), for serving
fresh guacamole with lime & garlic (page 44),
    for serving

In a small bowl, mix the achiote with the pepper, salt, orange zest, juice, and oil. Brush mixture all over the lamb. Let rest at room temperature for 1 hour.

Prepare an indirect fire in your grill — the coals or heat to one side and no heat on the other side. Place the lamb on the indirect side, cover, and grill for 1 1/2–2 hours or until a meat thermometer inserted in the thickest part registers 135–140°F for medium-rare.

To serve, let the lamb rest for 10 minutes, then carve into slices. Serve with warm flour tortillas and guacamole.

Serves 6–8

variations

pork carnitas

see base recipe page 143

lamb carnitas
Prepare the basic recipe, using boneless lamb shoulder in place of pork.
Serve topped with crumbled queso fresco and chopped fresh mint.

cabrito carnitas
Prepare the basic recipe, using boneless cabrito shoulder in place of pork.
Serve on mini corn or flour tortillas drizzled with a little smoky barbecue
sauce for a Tex-Mex appetizer.

beef carnitas
Prepare the basic recipe, using boneless beef chuck in place of pork.
Serve this on a bolillo or hard roll, with your favorite toppings, as a torta
or sandwich.

mayan-style roast pork in banana leaves

see base recipe page 144

mayan-style roast chicken in banana leaves
Prepare the basic recipe, using a whole roasting chicken in place of pork.
Indirect grill for 1 hour, then wrap in banana leaves (a large paper grocery
bag makes a good substitue for banana leaves—just put the meat in the bag
and fold the open end closed) and finish in the oven for 1 more hour.

mayan-style roast whole fish in banana leaves
Prepare the basic recipe, using a whole, cleaned fish in place of pork. Rub it
with the seasoning mixture, then wrap in banana leaves and indirect grill for
1 1/2 hours or until the fish flakes when tested with a fork.

mayan-style roast lamb in banana leaves
Prepare the basic recipe, using 4 racks of lamb ribs in place of pork.
Indirect grill for 2 hours, then wrap in banana leaves and finish in the oven
for 1 more hour.

mayan-style roast cabrito in banana leaves
Prepare the basic recipe, using 1 leg of cabrito in place of pork. Indirect grill
for 2 hours, then wrap in banana leaves and finish in the oven for 2 more
hours or until tender.

chorizo with eggs & potatoes

see base recipe page 146

pork carnitas with eggs & potatoes
Prepare the basic recipe, using pork carnitas (page 143) in place of chorizo and chopped fresh green chiles in place of the raisins.

costillar asado with eggs & potatoes
Why not serve leftover spare ribs for breakfast? Prepare the basic recipe, omitting the chorizo and raisins. Warm the spare ribs (page 148) in the oven. Serve on the side, as you would breakfast sausage or bacon.

carne asada with eggs & potatoes
Have some leftover steak for breakfast. Prepare the basic recipe, omitting the chorizo and raisins. Warm the carne asada (page 122) in the microwave or a hot skillet to accompany the eggs and potatoes.

costillar asado

see base recipe page 148

mexican barbecued beef ribs
Prepare the basic recipe, using beef ribs in place of baby backs and ground chipotle in place of oregano. Marinate the ribs in Mexican beer for up to 12 hours, then pat dry, season, and grill as directed.

mexican barbecued lamb ribs
Prepare the basic recipe, using lamb ribs in place of baby backs. Marinate the lamb ribs in pineapple juice for up to 2 hours, then pat dry, season, and grill as directed.

mexican barbecued cabrito ribs
Prepare the basic recipe, using cabrito ribs in place of baby backs. Marinate the ribs in bottled chipotle marinade for up to 2 hours, then pat dry, season, and grill as directed.

pork & green chile pozole

see base recipe page 150

chicken & green chile pozole
Prepare the basic recipe, using 5 pounds cut-up chicken in place of pork.

lamb & green chile pozole
Prepare the basic recipe, using boneless lamb shoulder in place of pork.

turkey & green chile pozole
Prepare the basic recipe, using 5 pounds turkey legs in place of pork.

cabrito & green chile pozole
Prepare the basic recipe, using 5 pounds cabrito leg in place of pork.

pork & poblano tamales

see base recipe page 153

chile & cheese tamales
Prepare the basic recipe, using cream cheese in place of pork.

turkey picadillo tamales
Prepare the basic recipe, using turkey empanadas filling (page 51) in place of
the pork filling.

fresh corn tamales
Prepare the basic recipe, using fresh corn kernels in place of pork.

tamales rapidos
Prepare the basic recipe, using 24 (6-inch) squares of aluminum foil in place
of soaked and drained cornhusks.

variations

pork chops in green mole

see base recipe page 154

pork chops in yellow mole
Prepare the basic recipe, using yellow mole (page 18) in place of green mole.

pork chops in chipotle sauce
Prepare the basic recipe, using chipotle sauce in place of green mole.
To make the sauce, blend 1 cup tomato-based barbecue sauce with 2 finely chopped canned chipotles in adobo sauce and 1 cup Mexican beer.

pork chops in pumpkin seed salsa
Prepare the basic recipe, using pumpkin seed salsa (page 25) in place of green mole.

pork chops in doctored-up mole
Prepare the basic recipe, using doctored-up mole (page 19) in place of green mole.

guava-glazed leg of lamb

see base recipe page 156

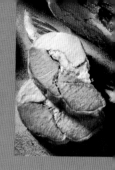

pineapple-glazed leg of lamb
Prepare the basic recipe, using pineapple preserves in place of guava jelly.
Serve with pineapple salsa (page 20).

margarita-glazed leg of lamb
Prepare the basic recipe, using margarita jelly in place of guava jelly. Garnish
with fresh lime and orange.

mango-glazed leg of lamb
Prepare the basic recipe, using mango jelly in place of guava jelly. Serve with
mango and lime salsa (page 22).

prickly pear-glazed leg of lamb
Prepare the basic recipe, using prickly pear cactus jelly in place of guava jelly.

variations

braised lamb shanks with tequila & chiles

see base recipe page 157

braised lamb shanks in mexican beer
Prepare the basic recipe, using Mexican beer in place of tequila.

wine-braised lamb shanks
Prepare the basic recipe, using dry red wine in place of tequila.

braised lamb shanks in mexican chocolate
Prepare the basic recipe, using Mexican hot chocolate (page 270) in place of
brewed coffee.

sangria-braised lamb shanks
Prepare the basic recipe, using sangria (page 263) in place of tequila and
2 jalapeños in place of canned chipotles in adobo.

veracruz–style grilled leg of lamb

see base recipe page 159

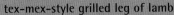

tex-mex–style grilled leg of lamb
Prepare the basic recipe, using 1 cup bottled ranch dressing in place of the
vegetable oil, orange zest, and orange juice, and adding 1 teaspoon ground
cumin and 1 teaspoon ground dried ancho chile to the marinade.

baja-style grilled leg of lamb
Prepare the basic recipe, using lime zest and lime juice in place of the orange
zest and juice.

oaxaca-style grilled leg of lamb
Prepare the basic recipe, using basic mole (page 17) in place of the marinade.

guadalajara-style grilled leg of lamb
Prepare the basic recipe, replacing the marinade with a mixture of 1/4 cup red
wine vinegar, 1/4 cup olive oil, 1 teaspoon ground cumin, 1 tablespoon ground
dried ancho chile, 1 teaspoon dried oregano, and salt and pepper to taste.

fish & shellfish

From the warm waters of the Gulf of Mexico and the Caribbean to the chillier waters of the Pacific, Mexico is blessed with miles of coastline and a wealth of fish and shellfish: shrimp, red snapper, and grouper from the Gulf and langosto or lobsters, flounder, swordfish, tuna, and yellow snapper from the Pacific.

mexican seafood stew

see variations page 188

Pescado (fish) and mariscos (shellfish) from both the Gulf and Pacific Coasts of Mexico go into this one-dish meal known as zarzuela.

1/2 cup vegetable oil
2 cups chopped onion
1/2 cup chopped fresh Italian parsley
1 cup long- or short-grain rice
1 (14 1/2-oz.) can chopped tomatoes, with liquid
1 cup clam juice
1 cup water
1/4 cup chopped fresh cilantro

1 lb. boneless, skinless fish fillets, such as halibut, grouper, or monkfish, cut into 1-inch pieces
1/2 lb. small bay scallops
1/2 lb. large uncooked shrimp, peeled and deveined
fresh avocado slices and lime wedges, to garnish

Heat the oil in a large pot over medium-high heat. Sauté the onion, stirring, until transparent, about 5 minutes. Stir in the parsley and rice and cook, stirring, until the rice begins to brown. Stir in the tomatoes, clam juice, and water. Bring to a boil, then reduce the heat, cover, and simmer for 15 minutes. Reduce the heat to low and stir in the cilantro, fish, scallops, and shrimp. Cover and cook for 10 minutes or until fish and shellfish are opaque. Serve in bowls, garnished with avocado slices and lime wedges.

Serves 4

baja fish tacos

see variations page 189

With a pitcher of margaritas or a frosty Mexican beer, enjoy the fresh flavor of these grilled fish tacos and all the authentic Baja fixings: red cabbage slaw, pico de gallo, and avocado cream. Use whatever mild, white-fleshed fish is freshest.

1/2 head red cabbage, cored and thinly sliced
2 tbsp. white vinegar
salt and pepper
2 ripe avocados, peeled and pitted
1/2 cup sour cream
2 tbsp. fresh lime juice

6 skinless mahimahi, pompano, yellow snapper, halibut, or cod fillets
vegetable oil for brushing
warm flour tortillas, for serving
pico de gallo (page 15), for serving

For the red cabbage slaw, combine the red cabbage and vinegar in a medium bowl and season to taste. For the avocado cream, purée the avocado, sour cream, and lime juice in a food processor or blender; season to taste.

Prepare a hot fire in your grill. Brush the fish with vegetable oil, then season to taste. Measure how thick the fish is in the thickest part (it's usually about 3/4-inch). Grill the fish, turning once, for 10 minutes per inch of thickness (about 7 1/2 minutes for a 3/4-inch-thick fillet).

To serve, cut the fish into strips and place in tortillas, garnished with the slaw, avocado cream, and pico de gallo.

Serves 6

grilled margarita-glazed fish

see variations page 190

Margaritas are delicious for drinking, but they're also great as a marinade and glaze for fish, shellfish, and chicken on the grill.

1 cup world's best margarita (page 255)
6 skinless mahimahi, pompano, halibut, or cod
   fillets

vegetable oil for brushing
salt and pepper

Place the fish fillets on a baking sheet and brush with half the margarita. Let sit at room temperature for 30 minutes.

Prepare a hot fire in your grill. Brush the fish with vegetable oil, then season to taste. Measure how thick the fish is in the thickest part (it's usually about 3/4 inch). Grill the fish, turning once and basting with the remaining margarita, for 10 minutes per inch of thickness (about 7 1/2 minutes for a 3/4-inch-thick fillet).

Serves 6

grilled shrimp skewers borrachos

see variations page 191

Marinated in Mexican beer — hence the "drunken" or borrachos in the title — then grilled to perfection, these skewers can be served with Mexican confetti rice (page 210), slow-simmered black beans (page 208), and authentic guacamole (page 30).

1 (12-oz.) bottle Mexican beer
3 cloves garlic, minced
2 tbsp. fresh lime juice
1 lb. large, raw shrimp, peeled and deveined

8 wooden skewers, soaked in water for at least
   30 minutes and drained
vegetable oil for brushing
salt and pepper

Place the beer, garlic, and lime juice in a sealable plastic bag. Add the shrimp. Seal the bag and let marinate for 30–60 minutes in the refrigerator. Remove the shrimp from the bag and thread onto the skewers without crowding; discard the marinade. Brush the shrimp with vegetable oil and season to taste.

Prepare a medium-hot fire in your grill. Grill the skewers for 2–3 minutes per side or until the shrimp are opaque and have good grill marks. Place 2 skewers on each serving plate.

Serves 4

grilled fish tostadas with pineapple-lime salsa

see variations page 192

A tostada is a flour tortilla layered with different ingredients, like a pizza.

2 cups chopped fresh pineapple
2 tbsp. fresh lime juice
1/4 tsp. dried crushed red pepper flakes
4 (9- to 10-inch) flour tortillas, homemade
    (page 16) or store-bought
vegetable oil for frying and brushing

4 white-fleshed fish fillets, such as mahimahi,
    halibut, monkfish, or cod
1 tsp. ground dried ancho or chipotle chile
salt and pepper
1 recipe avocado cream (page 172)
4 cups shredded lettuce

For the salsa, combine the pineapple, lime juice, and red pepper flakes in a bowl. Cover and refrigerate.

For the tostadas, heat 1/2-inch of vegetable oil in a large skillet over medium-high heat. Fry the flour tortillas, one at a time, until golden brown on both sides. Transfer to paper towels to drain and cool.

Prepare a hot fire in your grill. Brush the fish fillets with oil and season with ancho chile, salt, and pepper. Measure how thick the fish is at the thickest part (it's usually about 3/4 inch). Grill the fish, turning once, for 10 minutes per inch of thickness (about 7 1/2 minutes for a 3/4-inch-thick fillet). To serve, spread each tostada with avocado cream and sprinkle with 1 cup shredded lettuce. Top with a fish fillet and a quarter of the salsa.

Serves 4

banana leaf–wrapped fish fillets on the grill

see variations page 193

Leaf-wrapping foods is an ancient rainforest cooking method which was popular with both Mayan and Incan cultures. The leaves allow the fish to stay moist, delicious, and gently flavored. You can find banana leaves, fresh and frozen — as well as fresh avocado leaves and corn husks — at markets specializing in Hispanic products. Serve these fillets with slow-simmered black beans (page 208) and Mexican confetti rice (page 210).

1 frozen and thawed banana leaf, cut into 4
  pieces
4 (6-oz.) mahimahi, halibut, monkfish, or salmon
  fillets

salt and pepper
1 cup salsa of your choice

Lay each piece of banana leaf on a flat surface. Place a fish fillet in the center. Season to taste and top with 1/4 cup salsa. Carefully wrap the fish with the banana leaf.

Prepare a medium-hot fire in your grill or preheat the oven to 350°F. Place the banana leaf parcels on the grill or in the oven, close the lid or the door, and let cook for 16-20 minutes or until the fish flakes when tested with a fork. Remove from the grill or oven. Serve, allowing each diner to unwrap his or her own serving at the table.

Serves 4

tequila lime-grilled scallops

see variations page 194

With a brush of a margarita-like baste, sweet and meaty scallops take on fiesta flavor.

24 large sea scallops

for the marinade
1/2 cup olive oil
1/4 cup tequila
1/4 cup fresh lime juice

1 tsp. freshly grated lime zest
2 shallots, finely chopped
2 garlic cloves, minced
2 tsp. ground cumin
salt and pepper

Rinse the scallops and pat dry. In a bowl, combine the olive oil, tequila, lime juice, zest, shallots, garlic, and cumin. Season to taste. Place the scallops in a sealable plastic bag with half the tequila marinade. Reserve the other half. Seal the bag and shake to blend. Let marinate in the refrigerator for 30–60 minutes.

Prepare a hot fire in your grill. Remove the scallops from the marinade and broil, turning once, for 2–3 minutes per side or until opaque and with good grill marks. Serve drizzled with the remaining marinade.

Serves 6–8

lobster tacos with yellow tomato salsa

see variations page 195

Warm lobster tails on the grill outdoors or in a grill pan inside, then chop up the sweet meat and enjoy a taco vibrant with flavor, color, and texture.

for the salsa
2 cups halved yellow pear tomatoes or diced large yellow tomatoes
2 serrano chiles, stemmed, seeded, and diced
1/4 cup finely chopped green onion
8 oz. frozen and thawed lobster tails, shells removed

vegetable oil for brushing
salt and pepper
1 cup finely shredded lettuce
1 cup guacamole (homemade, page 30, or store-bought)
8 packaged taco shells

For the salsa, combine the tomatoes, chiles, and green onion in a bowl, and set aside.

Prepare a medium-hot fire in your grill or heat a grill pan over high heat indoors. Brush the lobster tails with vegetable oil and season to taste. Grill for 2–3 minutes per side or until they have good grill marks. Remove lobster tails and chop the meat.

Portion the lettuce among the taco shells, then top with a dollop of guacamole and some of the warm lobster meat. Serve with the salsa.

Serves 4

camarones a la diabla

see variations page 196

Hot and spicy, this deviled shrimp dish makes great party food, served over steamed white rice.

2 ancho or poblano chiles, stemmed and seeded
1 Anaheim chile, stemmed and seeded
2 serrano chiles, stemmed and seeded
2 cups chopped canned tomatoes, with liquid
3 tbsp. oil
3 tbsp. butter
1/2 onion, thinly sliced lengthwise

4 cloves garlic, minced
4 lbs. large uncooked shrimp, peeled and
  deveined
1 tbsp. Worcestershire sauce
2 tbsp. chicken broth
1/4 cup white wine
salt and pepper

Place the chiles in a saucepan with enough water to cover. Bring to a boil, then reduce the heat and simmer until tender, about 5 minutes. Drain and place the chiles in a food processor or blender with the tomatoes. Purée and set aside.

In a large pot, heat the oil and butter over medium-high heat. Sauté the onion and garlic until transparent, about 4 minutes. Add the shrimp and sauté until just barely pink and opaque, about 3 minutes. Stir in the Worcestershire sauce, chicken broth, wine, and tomato-chile purée, then season to taste and bring to a simmer. Serve over steamed white rice.

Serves 6-8

red snapper veracruzano

see variations page 197

Dishes in the Veracruz style often feature capers, tomatoes, and olives—a signature style that blends Spanish seasonings with local Mexican ingredients.

4 red snapper, mahimahi, or halibut fillets (about 8 oz. each)
1 recipe salsa cruda (page 21) or 2 cups store-bought fresh salsa
1/4 tsp. ground white pepper

1 tsp. ground cinnamon
1/2 cup sliced pimiento-stuffed olives
1/4 cup olive oil
capers, to garnish

Preheat the oven to 400°F. Place the fish fillets in a baking dish. In a bowl, combine the salsa, white pepper, cinnamon, olives, and olive oil. Spoon this mixture over the fish. Bake for 15 minutes or until the fish is just beginning to flake.

To serve, place the fish and sauce on plates and garnish with capers.

Serves 4

variations

mexican seafood stew

see base recipe page 171

shellfish stew in cilantro-saffron
Prepare the basic recipe, adding 1 teaspoon saffron threads to the water and using fresh clams or mussels in place of fish. (Do not use any clams or mussels that have opened before cooking and discard any that do not open after cooking.)

seafood stew with squash, tomatoes & saffron
Prepare the basic recipe, adding 1 teaspoon saffron threads to the water and 1 cup diced zucchini or yellow summer squash with the seafood.

seafood stew in roasted poblano broth
Prepare the basic recipe, adding 1 cup roasted, stemmed, seeded, and chopped poblano chile to the broth after browning the rice.

smoky mexican seafood stew
Prepare the basic recipe, adding 1/4 cup bottled smoked chipotle sauce when you add the cilantro, fish, scallops, and shrimp.

baja fish tacos

see base recipe page 172

baja shrimp tacos
Prepare the basic recipe, using grilled shrimp in place of fish.

baja chicken tacos
Prepare the basic recipe, using slices of grilled, boneless, skinless chicken breasts in place of fish.

baja swordfish tacos
Prepare the basic recipe, using grilled swordfish steaks seasoned with smoked paprika in place of fish.

baja vegetarian tacos
Prepare the basic recipe, using grilled tofu in place of fish.

variations

grilled margarita-glazed fish

see base recipe page 174

grilled margarita-glazed fish with salsa fresca
Prepare the basic recipe, then serve with a fresh salsa made with 2 cups chopped mango or papaya, 2 tablespoons fresh lime juice, and 1/2 teaspoon dried red pepper flakes.

grilled margarita-glazed fish with grilled guacamole
Prepare the basic recipe, then serve with grilled guacamole (page 44).

grilled margarita-glazed fish with cilantro salsa
Prepare the basic recipe, then serve with cilantro salsa (page 26)

grilled margarita-glazed fish with tomatillo salsa
Prepare the basic recipe, then serve with tomatillo salsa (page 19).

grilled margarita-glazed pork with pineapple salsa
Prepare the basic recipe, using pork chops in place of fish fillets. Serve with pineapple salsa (page 20).

variations

grilled shrimp skewers borrachos

see base recipe page 176

grilled shrimp skewers in margarita marinade
Prepare the basic recipe, using 1 cup world's best margarita (page 255) in place of the beer, garlic, and lime juice marinade. Marinate for only 30 minutes, then grill.

grilled shrimp skewers in citrus mojo
Prepare the basic recipe, using 1 cup bottled citrus mojo marinade in place of the beer, garlic, and lime juice marinade.

grilled shrimp skewers with cilantro salsa
Prepare the basic recipe, then serve with cilantro salsa (page 26).

grilled chicken skewers borrachos
Prepare the basic recipe, using boneless, skinless chicken breast cut into 2-inch pieces in place of shrimp.

variations

grilled fish tostadas with pineapple-lime salsa

see base recipe page 179

grilled fish tostadas with papaya-lime salsa
Prepare the basic recipe, using papaya in place of pineapple.

grilled chicken tostadas with papaya-lime salsa
Prepare the basic recipe, using boneless, skinless chicken breast in place of
fish and papaya in place of pineapple.

pork carnitas tostadas with papaya-lime salsa
Prepare the basic recipe, using pork carnitas (page 143) in place of fish and
papaya in place of pineapple.

crab & black bean tostadas with papaya-lime salsa
Prepare the basic recipe, using a mixture of 1 cup rinsed canned black beans,
1 cup cooked crabmeat, 1/2 teaspoon ground cumin, 1/2 cup Mexican crèma
or sour cream in place of the seasoned fish and papaya in place of pineapple.

banana leaf–wrapped fish fillets on the grill

see base recipe page 180

avocado leaf–wrapped fish fillets on the grill

Prepare the basic recipe, using fresh avocado leaves, soaked in hot water until pliable and then dried, in place of banana leaf.

cornhusk–wrapped fish fillets on the grill

Prepare the basic recipe, using fresh cornhusks in place of banana leaf. If using dried cornhusks, soak them in hot water for several hours, then drain and pat dry.

parchment paper–wrapped fish fillets on the grill

Prepare the basic recipe, using squares of parchment paper in place of banana leaf.

banana leaf-wrapped pork on the grill

Prepare the basic recipe, using sliced pork loin in place of fish fillets.

variations

tequila lime-grilled scallops

see base recipe page 182

tequila lime-grilled shrimp
Prepare the basic recipe, using 2 pounds peeled and deveined large shrimp in place of scallops.

tequila lime-grilled salmon
Prepare the basic recipe, using 2 pounds salmon fillet in place of scallops.

tequila lime-grilled sea bass
Prepare the basic recipe, using 2 pounds sea bass fillet in place of scallops.

tequila lime-grilled swordfish
Prepare the basic recipe, using 2 pounds swordfish steak in place of scallops.

variations

lobster tacos with yellow tomato salsa

see base recipe page 183

salmon tacos with yellow & green tomato salsa
Prepare the basic recipe, using 1/2 pound grilled salmon fillet in place of
lobster and adding 1/2 cup husked and chopped fresh tomatillos to the salsa.

shrimp tacos with yellow tomato salsa
Prepare the basic recipe, using 1/2 pound grilled shrimp in place of lobster.

tuna tacos with yellow & green tomato salsa
Prepare the basic recipe, using 1/2 pound grilled tuna steak in place of lobster
and adding 1/2 cup husked and chopped fresh tomatillos to the salsa.

swordfish tacos with pumpkin seed salsa
Prepare the basic recipe, using 1/2 pound grilled swordfish steaks in place
of lobster and pumpkin seed salsa (page 25) in place of yellow tomato salsa.

variations

camarones a la diabla

see base recipe page 184

vieiras a la diabla
Prepare the basic recipe, using sea scallops in place of shrimp.

yellow-fin tuna a la diabla
Prepare the basic recipe, using yellow-fin tuna steak, cut into 2-inch pieces, in place of shrimp.

swordfish a la diabla
Prepare the basic recipe, using swordfish steaks, cut into 2-inch pieces, in place of shrimp.

chicken a la diabla
Prepare the basic recipe, using 2-inch pieces of boneless, skinless chicken breasts in place of shrimp.

red snapper veracruzano

see base recipe page 186

baja-style red snapper
Prepare the basic recipe, using a Baja-style sauce instead of the Veracruzano sauce. Mix 1/4 cup olive oil, 1/2 cup chopped green onions, 1/4 cup chopped fresh Italian parsley, 1 cup chopped ripe tomato, and the juice of 1 lime. Spread it over the fish before baking.

yucatán-style red snapper
Prepare the basic recipe, adding 1/2 teaspoon freshly grated orange zest and 1/2 cup orange juice to the sauce. Spread it over the fish before baking.

red snapper escabeche
Prepare the basic recipe. Transfer the fish to a serving platter and let come to room temperature. To the sauce in the baking dish, stir in 2 tablespoons white vinegar and 2 tablespoons fresh orange juice. Pour the pan juice mixture over the fish and chill. Serve cold.

grill-baked red snapper
Prepare the basic recipe, but use a grill-proof metal pan instead of a baking dish. Prepare an indirect fire in your grill. Place the pan on the indirect side, close the lid, and grill-bake for 20-30 minutes or until the fish is just beginning to flake.

vegetables

Vegetables, fresh and in season, become zesty accompaniments to Mexican entrees or stand-alone dishes. Many of these recipes are family favorites, such as chiles rellenos, served at holiday time. Others take advantage of whatever is in season in the garden or at the mercado.

chiles rellenos

see variations page 218

Fresh-roasted Anaheim or poblano chiles are stuffed with cheese and then fried in an egg batter in this classic dish from Puebla, just east of Mexico City.

8 fresh Anaheim or poblano chiles
1 lb. Chihuahua, Asadero, or Monterey Jack
   cheese, cut to fit inside the chiles
1/2 cup all-purpose flour
2 tbsp. olive oil
1/2 cup chopped onion

1 clove garlic, minced
1 (15-oz.) can tomato purée
1 tbsp. chopped fresh epazote or oregano leaves
salt and pepper to taste
vegetable oil for frying
3 large eggs, separated

Place the chiles on a baking sheet under the broiler and broil, turning them over once, until the skins are blackened. Place the chiles in a plastic bag, close, and let them steam for 5 minutes. Remove the skins under cold, running water. Keeping the stems intact, slit each chile 3/4 down the length of one side. Carefully spoon out the interior ribs and seeds. Stuff each chile with a piece of cheese and roll in flour. Set aside.

Heat the olive oil in a saucepan over medium-high heat. Sauté the onion and garlic until golden. Stir in the tomato purée and oregano, season to taste, and set aside.

Pour the vegetable oil to a depth of 1 1/2 inches in a deep and wide frying pan and heat to 425°F. Beat the egg whites until stiff in a large bowl. Beat the yolks until blended, then fold the whites and yolks together. Working in batches, dip each stuffed chile in the egg batter, then fry in the hot oil for 2–3 minutes or until lightly browned. Remove from heat, drain on paper towels. Serve topped with the tomato sauce.

Serves 4–6

black bean & roasted tomato tamales

see variations page 219

This vegetarian version of tamales has wonderful color and flavor. "Tamal" is the singular of tamales.

3 cups coarsely chopped yellow tomatoes
1 tbsp. olive oil
1 tbsp. fresh lime juice
salt and pepper to taste
1 (15-oz.) can black beans
2 cloves garlic, minced

1/2 tsp. ground cumin
1/2 tsp. dried epazote or oregano leaves
10 dried cornhusks, soaked in water for
    30 minutes and drained
1 1/2 cups instant corn masa flour
1 1/4 cups vegetable broth

Place the chopped tomatoes on a baking sheet and drizzle with olive oil. Roast at 450°F for 15 minutes or until blistered. Place in a blender or food processor with the lime juice and process until somewhat smooth. Season to taste and set aside.

In a saucepan, bring the black beans, garlic, cumin, and oregano to a boil over medium-high heat. Reduce the heat and simmer until thickened, about 15 minutes.

Arrange the cornhusks on a flat surface. Place the masa flour in a bowl. Stir in the broth to make a soft dough, adding a little more water if necessary. Divide the dough into 10 portions and form each portion into a ball. Place each ball of dough between two unopened plastic sandwich bags, then press to a 5- to 6-inch round in a tortilla press.

Place a tablespoon of roasted yellow tomato sauce and a tablespoon of black beans in the middle of each tortilla. Fold in the sides and place in the damp cornhusk. Fold the sides in, then the ends, to enclose the filling. Secure the ends with string so that each tamal is completely enclosed in the husk. Place the tamales vertically in a steamer; do not let them touch the water. Steam for 30 minutes or until the husks pull away from the filling. To serve, unwrap each tamal and serve with more roasted yellow tomato sauce.

Serves 4–6

sizzling mushroom fajitas

see variations page 220

Beef-tasting portabello mushrooms, in place of traditional beef or chicken, make delicious fajitas, too. Serve with store-bought or homemade flour tortillas (page 16), guacamole (page 30), and pico de gallo (page 15).

1 1/2 lbs. portabello mushrooms
1 large onion, sliced into 1-inch rounds
1 red bell pepper, stemmed, seeded, and
    cut into quarters
vegetable oil

salt and pepper to taste
flour tortillas, guacamole, and pico de gallo
    (store-bought or homemade), for serving

Prepare a hot fire in your grill or heat a cast-iron fajita pan on the stovetop until very hot. Brush the mushrooms, onion slices, and red bell pepper with vegetable oil and season to taste. Grill the onion and bell pepper for 5–7 minutes per side or until charred and softened. Grill the mushrooms for 1 1/2–2 minutes per side or until you have good grill marks. Slice the mushrooms on the diagonal and serve with the grilled vegetables, tortillas, guacamole, and pico de gallo.

Serves 4

fresh corn flan

see variations page 221

The Spanish conquistadors brought their love of flan to Mexico. Today, the most common flans are caramel custard and orange flan, but not all flans are sweet. These individual fresh corn flans make an easy yet elegant side dish. Pair them with the salsa of your choice as a sauce.

4 cups fresh or frozen and thawed corn kernels
1 1/2 cups half-and-half
6 large eggs
1 tsp. salt

1 tsp. ground dried ancho or chipotle chile or
   bottled chipotle sauce
salsa or mole of your choice

Preheat the oven to 350°F. Grease the insides of eight 6-oz. custard cups and place in a deep baking pan with enough hot water to come halfway up the sides of the cups. Place the corn in a food processor and process until smooth. Add the half-and-half, eggs, salt, and ground ancho, and process until smooth.

Divide the mixture among the prepared custard cups. Bake for 25 minutes or until a knife inserted in the center of a flan comes out clean. Loosen the flans with a knife and invert onto serving plates. Serve with the salsa or mole of your choice.

Serves 8

three sisters vegetable stew

see variations page 222

The "three sisters" — corn, beans, and squash — have been grown by indigenous Mexican peoples for thousands of years. The men slash and burn a plot and the women plant the seeds and tend the garden. The beans use the cornstalks for support. The squash helps repel weeds around both, so the "sisters" work harmoniously together, as in this recipe.

2 tbsp. olive oil
1 large onion, chopped
4 garlic cloves, minced
2 cups fresh or frozen and thawed corn kernels
2 cups chopped fresh or frozen and thawed
    butternut or acorn squash

1 large dried chipotle chile
4 cups vegetable or chicken broth
1 (15-oz.) can pinto beans, with their juice
salt and pepper to taste
chopped fresh Italian parsley and green onion,
    to garnish

Heat the oil in a large saucepan over medium-high heat. Sauté the onion and garlic until transparent, about 7 minutes. Stir in the corn, squash, chipotle, and broth. Bring to a boil, then reduce the heat and simmer for 15 minutes or until the squash and chipotle are tender. Remove the chipotle, chop finely, and return to the pan along with the pinto beans. Cook, stirring, until the stew is hot. Season to taste. Serve in bowls garnished with Italian parsley and chopped green onion.

Serves 4–6

slow-simmered black beans

see variations page 223

A pot of frijoles negras or black beans is often simmering in a Mexican kitchen, as these beans can feature as a side dish at any meal. They're also delicious turned into a salsa, soup, or a filling for a taco or burrito. Mexican cooks often add the herb epazote to beans as they're cooking; the herb adds a flavor similar to oregano and also aids in digesting the beans.

1/4 cup vegetable oil
1 large onion, chopped
2 cloves garlic, chopped
2 1/2 cups (about 1 lb.) dried black beans,
    picked over

1 tsp. dried epazote or oregano leaves, crumbled
8 cups water
1 tsp. bottled liquid smoke flavoring
salt

In a large pot over medium-high heat, heat the oil, add the onion and garlic, and sauté until the onion has softened, about 4 minutes. Stir in the beans, epazote, and water, and bring to a boil. Reduce the heat and simmer, covered, until the beans are tender, about 2 1/2 hours. If the beans are too soupy, continue to cook uncovered until thickened. Stir in the liquid smoke flavoring and season to taste.

Serves 6–8

frijoles refritos

see variations page 224

Although often seen on Mexican menus as "refried beans," these pinto beans are actually not fried but cooked in good-quality lard for an authentic flavor and texture. They're also popular as a side dish with any meal.

2 1/2 cups (about 1 lb.) dried pinto beans, picked over
1/2 cup chopped onion

1/2 cup lard or bacon drippings
salt

Place the beans in a large saucepan with enough cold water to cover them. Let stand at room temperature overnight. Drain, then place the beans back in the saucepan. Add the onion and enough water to just cover the beans. Bring to a boil, reduce the heat, and simmer, covered, until the beans are tender and will mash easily, about 2 1/2 hours. Remove from the heat and drain, reserving about 1 cup of the cooking liquid. With a potato masher, mash the beans in the pot until they are a blend of smooth and chunky. Add some of the cooking liquid if necessary. Stir in the lard and cook over medium-high heat, stirring constantly, until the fat has been absorbed and the beans are hot. Season to taste before serving.

Serves 6–8

mexican confetti rice

see variations page 225

Also called arroz a la Mexicana or Spanish rice, this dish rounds out any casual meal.

4 tbsp. vegetable oil
1 large onion, chopped
2 cloves garlic, minced
2 cups uncooked long-grain rice
1 (15-oz.) can peeled and chopped tomatoes,
    with liquid

1 (4-oz.) can green chiles
2 cups chicken broth
1/4 cup chopped firmly packed cilantro leaves

Heat the oil in a large saucepan over medium-high heat. Sauté the onion and garlic until softened, about 4 minutes. Stir in the rice until it is well coated by the onion/garlic mixture. Stir in the tomatoes, chiles, and chicken broth, and bring to a boil. Reduce the heat and simmer, covered, about 25 minutes, adding a little water if necessary, until the rice is tender and the liquid is absorbed. Remove from the heat, stir in the cilantro, and serve.

Serves 6–8

stuffed poblano chiles with walnut sauce

see variations page 226

Known as chiles en nogada, this classic dish is usually served to celebrate Mexican Independence Day as it has the colors of the Mexican flag — red, green, and white.

1 cup walnut pieces
3/4 cup sliced almonds
4 oz. cream cheese
1 cup half-and-half
1 tsp. sugar
1/2 cup sour cream or crèma

1/4 cup dry sherry
1/4 tsp. ground cinnamon
4 fresh poblano chiles
1 recipe empanada filling (page 42)
fresh parsley and pomegranate seeds, to garnish

First, make the walnut sauce. Place the walnut pieces in a bowl with water to cover and soak for 4 hours at room temperature. Drain the walnuts and place in a food processor with the almonds. Process until finely ground. Transfer the ground nuts to a saucepan over medium heat and stir in the cream cheese, half-and-half, and sugar. Stir until the cream cheese has melted and the mixture is well blended. Remove from the heat and stir in the sour cream, sherry, and cinnamon. Set aside. Place the poblanos on a baking sheet under the broiler, and broil, turning the chiles once, until the skins are blackened. Place the poblanos in a plastic bag, close, and leave for 5 minutes. Remove the skins under cold, running water. Keeping the stems intact, slit each chile 3/4 down the length of one side. Carefully spoon out the interior ribs and seeds. Stuff each chile with the empanada filling. Serve each stuffed chile accompanied by the walnut sauce. Sprinkle with Italian parsley and pomegranate seeds.

Serves 4

charcoal-grilled corn with chile–lime butter

see variations page 227

One of Mexico's great culinary gifts to the world is fresh, sweet corn. When it's at its peak in summer, try it the way mercado vendors like to serve it.

8 ears fresh corn in the husk
1/2 cup unsalted butter, softened
1 tbsp. ground dried chipotle

1 tsp. freshly grated lime zest
salt

Pull back the husks from each ear of corn and remove the corn silk. Pull the husks back over the corn and place in a large bowl of cold water. Soak for 30 minutes.

Mash the butter with the chipotle and lime zest until well blended.

Prepare a hot fire in your grill. Remove the corn from the water and drain. Slightly open the husks and brush some of the chile–lime butter on the corn kernels. Close the husk and tie the ends with strips of cornhusk or kitchen twine. Place the ears of corn directly over the fire and grill for 6–8 minutes, turning with tongs as the husks begin to brown. To serve, untie the ears, pull back the husks, and brush the kernels with more chile-lime butter.

Serves 4–6

cinco de mayo grilled vegetable platter with salsa verde

see variations page 228

Cinco de Mayo, Spanish for the "5th of May," is a Mexican national holiday celebrating the victory over the French at Puebla de Los Angeles in 1862. Foods in the colors of the Mexican flag — red, green, and white — are popular.

for the salsa verde
1 (13-oz.) can tomatillos, with liquid
1 large onion, peeled and quartered
1 clove garlic
1 (4-oz.) can green chiles
for the vegetables
2 large yellow onions, peeled and sliced 1/2-inch thick

2 bunches green onions, trimmed
4 large tomatoes, stemmed, cored, and cut into 1-inch-thick slices
olive oil for brushing
salt and pepper
fresh cilantro, to garnish

To make the salsa verde, place the tomatillos, onion, garlic, and green chiles in a blender or food processor. Process until smooth and set aside.

Prepare a hot fire in your grill. Brush the vegetables with olive oil and season to taste with salt and pepper. Grill, turning, until you have good grill marks. Arrange the vegetables on a serving platter. Drizzle with salsa verde, garnish with cilantro, and serve.

Serves 8

grilled poblano & onion strips

see variations page 229

Known as rajas or rags, these strips make a delicious accompaniment to beef dishes of all kinds, as well as a filling for sandwiches, burritos, tacos, enchiladas, or quesadillas.

4 fresh poblano chiles
olive oil for brushing
2 large yellow onions, peeled and cut into
    1/2-inch slices
salt and pepper to taste

Prepare a hot fire in your grill.

Brush the poblanos with olive oil and grill, turning often, until the skins blister and burn. Transfer to a sealable plastic bag and let them steam and soften. Brush the onions with olive oil and grill until you have good grill marks on both sides, about 10 minutes total. Remove the stems, skin, and seeds from the poblanos, then slice into thin strips. Cut the onion slices in half and break apart with a fork into strands. Combine the poblanos and onions and season to taste. Keep the rajas warm until serving.

Serves 4–6

variations

chiles rellenos

see base recipe page 199

chiles rellenos picadillo
Prepare the basic recipe, using empanada filling (page 42) in place of cheese.

grill-roasted chiles rellenos
Prepare the basic recipe, using the barbecue grill, instead of the broiler, to roast the chiles before proceeding with the recipe.

stuffed jalapeños
Prepare the basic recipe, using 24 fresh jalapeños in place of poblanos.

chiles rellenos en nogada
Prepare the basic recipe without the tomato sauce. Top the filled chiles with the walnut sauce.

black bean & roasted tomato tamales

see base recipe page 200

wild mushroom tamales
Prepare the basic recipe, using 2 cups sautéed wild mushrooms in place of black beans.

smoked vegetable tamales
Prepare the basic recipe, using 2 cups sautéed vegetables seasoned with 1 teaspoon liquid smoke in place of black beans.

smoky cheese & herb tamales
Prepare the basic recipe, using 2 cups grated smoked mozzarella mixed with 1/4 cup fresh chopped cilantro in place of black beans.

picadillo tamales
Prepare the basic recipe, using 2 cups empanada filling (page 42) in place of black beans.

variations

sizzling mushroom fajitas

see base recipe page 202

sizzling vegetable fajitas
Prepare the basic recipe, using strips of fresh zucchini, cut 1/2-inch thick, in place of mushrooms.

sizzling corn fajitas
Prepare the basic recipe, using 4 ears of fresh corn, grilled on all sides, in place of mushrooms. With a paring knife, remove the grilled corn kernels and mix with the grilled vegetables.

sizzling black bean fajitas
Prepare the basic recipe, using 2 cups warm canned black beans in place of grilled mushrooms.

sizzling salmon fajitas
Grill a 1-pound skinless salmon fillet, brushed on both sides with olive oil, over a hot fire for 4 minutes per side as you're grilling the vegetables. Cut the salmon into pieces and serve in the tortillas. Top with grilled vegetables and a dollop of authentic guacamole (page 30).

variations

fresh corn flan

see base recipe page 205

fresh squash flan
Prepare the basic recipe, using cooked butternut or acorn squash in place of corn.

fresh pumpkin flan
Prepare the basic recipe, using cooked pumpkin in place of corn.

fresh hominy flan
Prepare the basic recipe, using canned, drained hominy in place of corn.

roasted vegetable & goat cheese flan
Prepare the basic recipe, using 3 cups roasted vegetables and 1 cup fresh goat cheese in place of corn.

fresh zucchini flan
Prepare the basic recipe, replacing the corn with cooked zucchini.

variations

three sisters vegetable stew

see base recipe page 206

three sisters vegetable & chorizo stew
Prepare the basic recipe, adding 1 pound cooked and chopped chorizo to the stew with the pinto beans.

three sisters vegetable & pork stew
Prepare the basic recipe, adding 2 cups pork carnitas (page 143) to the stew with the pinto beans.

three sisters grilled-vegetable stew
Grill a bunch of green onions and 2 medium zucchini, then chop. Prepare the basic recipe, adding the onion and zucchini in place of the butternut squash.

three sisters summer vegetable stew
Prepare the basic recipe, adding 1 cup chopped zucchini and 1 cup chopped yellow summer squash in place of butternut, then proceed with the recipe.

variations

slow-simmered black beans

see base recipe page 208

slow-simmered teppary beans
Prepare the basic recipe, using dried teppary beans in place of black beans.

slow-simmered chipotle black beans
Prepare the basic recipe, adding 2 canned chipotles in adobo, chopped, to the onion and garlic.

pantry shelf black beans
Heat 2 (15-oz.) cans black beans, drained, in a saucepan with 1/2 cup finely chopped onion, 1/2 cup finely chopped boiled ham, 1 teaspoon chopped garlic, and 1 teaspoon dried oregano or epazote. Bring to a simmer and cook for 15 minutes to let the flavors blend. Season to taste with salt and pepper.

moors & christians
Prepare the basic recipe, serving the black beans over coconut rice (page 225).

variations

frijoles refritos

see base recipe page 209

vegetarian frijoles refritos
Prepare the basic recipe, using 1/2 cup vegetable oil in place of lard.

pantry shelf frijoles refritos
Heat 2 (15-oz.) cans pinto beans, drained, in a saucepan with 1/2 cup finely
chopped onion and 1/2 cup lard. Bring to a simmer and cook for 15 minutes
to let the flavors blend. Season to taste with salt and pepper.

black beans refritos
Prepare the basic recipe, replacing half the quantity of pinto beans with
black beans.

mexican confetti rice

see base recipe page 210

vegetarian confetti rice
Prepare the basic recipe, using vegetable broth in place of chicken broth and proceed with the recipe.

confetti rice ole!
Prepare the basic recipe, using 1 stemmed, seeded, and chopped small jalapeño in place of canned, and adding 1/4 cup chopped fresh yellow bell pepper and 1/4 cup chopped fresh orange bell pepper.

ancho confetti rice
Prepare the basic recipe, adding 1 teaspoon dried ground ancho chile to the chicken broth.

coconut rice
Prepare the basic recipe, using 1/2 cup flaked fresh or dried coconut (not sweetened flaked coconut) in place of the tomatoes and 1/2 cup cream of coconut in place of the chiles. (This is traditionally served with slow-simmered black beans or fish dishes.)

variations

stuffed poblano chiles with walnut sauce

see base recipe page 212

stuffed poblano chiles with pumpkin seed salsa
Prepare the basic recipe, using pumpkin seed salsa (page 25) in place of walnut sauce.

stuffed poblano chiles with yellow tomato salsa
Prepare the basic recipe, using yellow tomato salsa (page 183) in place of walnut sauce.

stuffed poblano chiles with salsa cruda
Prepare the basic recipe, using salsa cruda (page 21) in place of walnut sauce.

fried stuffed poblano chiles
Prepare the basic recipe without the walnut sauce. Separate 3 large eggs. Pour vegetable oil to a depth of 1 1/2 inches in a deep and wide frying pan and heat to 425°F. Beat the egg whites until stiff in a large bowl. Beat the yolks until blended, then fold the whites and yolks together. Dip each stuffed chile in the egg batter and fry in hot oil for 2–3 minutes or until lightly browned.

charcoal-grilled corn with chile-lime butter

see base recipe page 213

charcoal-grilled chiles with chile-lime butter
Prepare the basic recipe, using 4 Anaheim and 4 poblano chiles in place of corn. Grill the peppers whole, turning often, until blistered on all sides. Stem, seed, and slice. Serve with the butter.

charcoal-grilled potatoes with chile-lime butter
Prepare the basic recipe, using 4 baking potatoes in place of corn. Prick the potatoes all over and par-cook in the microwave for 5 minutes. Cut lengthwise into 1/2-inch slices and brush with some of the butter. Grill for 2-3 minutes per side or until done. Serve with the remaining butter.

charcoal-grilled mixed vegetables with chile-lime butter
Prepare the basic recipe, using 2 medium yellow summer squash and 2 medium zucchini in place of corn. Trim the ends of the squash, slice in half lengthwise, and brush with some of the butter. Grill for 2-3 minutes per side or until you have good grill marks. Serve with the remaining butter.

variations

cinco de mayo grilled vegetable platter
with salsa verde

see base recipe page 214

cinco de mayo grilled vegetable platter with chile–lime butter
Prepare the basic recipe, using melted chile-lime butter (page 213) in place of salsa verde.

cinco de mayo grilled vegetable platter with chipotle–lime vinaigrette
Prepare the basic recipe, using chipotle–lime vinaigrette (page 69) drizzled over the salad in place of salsa verde.

cinco de mayo roasted vegetable platter with salsa verde
Prepare the basic recipe, placing the vegetables on a baking sheet in a 450°F oven until browned and blistered, about 20 minutes.

cinco de mayo grilled vegetable platter with pumpkin seed salsa
Prepare the basic recipe, using pumpkin seed salsa (page 25) in place of salsa verde.

grilled poblano & onion strips

see base recipe page 217

grilled whole poblanos & torpedo onions
Prepare the basic recipe, using large green or torpedo onions in place of yellow onions. Grill the torpedo onions whole, then slice into strips.

roasted poblano & onion strips
Prepare the basic recipe, placing the vegetables on a baking sheet in a 450°F oven until browned and blistered (about 20 minutes).

sautéed poblano & onion strips
Prepare the basic recipe, using stemmed, seeded, and sliced poblanos in place of whole poblanos. Heat the olive oil in a large skillet over medium-high heat and sauté the poblano strips and onion slices until browned and tender (about 10 minutes).

grilled bell pepper & onion strips
Prepare the basic recipe, using whole yellow and red bell peppers in place of whole poblanos.

desserts

In the easygoing Mexican culture, sweet things are for any time of day. Rice or bread pudding for breakfast. Bunuelos with a mug of warm champurrado on a chilly afternoon. Cakes, flans, and ice creams on festive occasions or simply after a family dinner.

bunuelos

see variations page 245

Flour tortillas, lightly fried in oil, are then dusted with cinnamon sugar for a simple, sweet finish to a meal. Served with warm chocolate champurrado (page 268), bunuelos are also one of the ways families welcome friends and loved ones during the holidays. For the best flavor, grind your own cinnamon in a clean coffee or spice grinder.

1 cup sugar
4 (3-inch) sticks cinnamon, ground in a coffee
   or spice grinder (or 1/4 cup
   ground cinnamon)

1 recipe homemade flour tortillas (page 16) or
   12 store-bought flour tortillas
vegetable oil for frying

Mix the sugar and ground cinnamon together in a bowl. Set aside.

Pour the vegetable oil into a deep frying pan to a depth of 1 inch. Heat the oil to 375°F. Fry the tortillas, 1 or 2 at a time, until golden brown and crisp, about 30–60 seconds per side. Remove with tongs, drain on paper towels, and sprinkle liberally on both sides with cinnamon sugar.

Makes 1 dozen

mexican wedding cookies

see variations page 246

Dusted with confectioners' sugar, these festive cookies are tender, buttery, and delicious. Grind the almonds in a food processor or a nut grinder before using.

1 1/2 cups (3 sticks) unsalted butter, softened
2 tbsp. confectioners' sugar
1 large egg yolk
1 tsp. vanilla extract

1/2 cup ground almonds
3 1/2 cups all-purpose flour
2 cups confectioners' sugar for dusting

Preheat the oven to 275°F. Line 2 baking sheets with parchment paper and set aside. In a mixing bowl, cream the butter and 2 tbsp. confectioners' sugar together with an electric mixer until light and fluffy. Beat in the egg yolk, vanilla, and almonds. Beat in the flour, a little at a time, until well blended. Pinch off tablespoon-size pieces of dough and roll into a ball. Place balls 2 inches apart on the prepared baking sheets. Bake for 45 minutes or until lightly browned. Let cool on the baking sheets until slightly warm.

Sift the remaining confectioners' sugar onto a sheet of parchment paper. Gently roll each cookie in the sugar until well coated. Store in airtight containers for up to 3 days.

Makes 3 dozen cookies

mango ice cream

see variations page 247

This fresh-tasting, easy-to-make frozen treat is just what you want on a hot day or after a spicy meal.

2 large, ripe mangoes, peeled, seeded, and
    chopped
1/2 cup sugar
1 cup heavy cream
1 tbsp. fresh lemon or lime juice

Place the mangoes, sugar, cream, and lemon juice in a food processor and process until smooth. Pour the mixture into an ice cream maker and freeze according to the manufacturer's directions.

Makes 2 pints

mexican rice pudding

see variations page 248

The Spanish conquistadors brought their love of rice dishes to Mexico in the 1500s. This comfort food classic, known as arroz con leche, is wonderful at any meal.

8 cups whole milk
1 cup sugar
1/4 tsp. salt
2 cinnamon sticks, plus 8 more for garnish
2 cups short-grain rice, rinsed

1 (14-oz.) can sweetened, condensed milk
1 tbsp. vanilla extract
1 cup dried fruit, such as golden raisins or dried mango, soaked in warm water to soften
1 (3.3-oz.) disk Mexican chocolate for grating

Place the milk, sugar, salt, and cinnamon sticks in a large saucepan, and bring to a boil over medium-high heat. Stir in the rice, reduce the heat, and simmer, covered, until tender, about 15 minutes. Remove from the heat and stir in the sweetened, condensed milk and vanilla. Drain the dried fruit and stir it into the rice pudding.

Serve the pudding warm or chilled, garnished with a cinnamon stick, and a dusting of grated Mexican chocolate.

Serves 8

passion fruit sorbet

see variations page 249

Many large supermarkets now carry frozen tropical fruit pulp, which makes it easy to get the flavor of Mexico in a frozen treat. Make a simple syrup of water and sugar, then blend in the frozen pulp and flavorings and freeze in an ice cream maker. Passion fruit, known as parcha in Mexico, are small, seedy fruits with a sweet-tart flavor.

1 cup water
1 cup sugar
1 (14-oz.) package passion fruit pulp, slightly
   thawed
1/4 tsp. freshly grated lime zest

2 tbsp. fresh lime juice
mint sprigs, to garnish (optional)

In a saucepan, bring the water and sugar to a boil, stirring until the sugar dissolves. Remove from the heat and let cool. Stir the passion fruit pulp, lime zest, and juice into the syrup. Pour the mixture into an ice cream maker and freeze according to manufacturer's directions.

Makes about 1 pint

hacienda-style flan

see variations page 250

Large acre estates known as haciendas usually concentrate on one regional agricultural product: agave for mescal and tequila in Zacatecas, sugar in Morelos, coffee in Oaxaca, sisal in Yucatán, and cattle in Querétaro. During the centuries of Spanish and French colonial rule, haciendas were the power bases of the gentry, with each known for the quality of its kitchen.

2 cups fresh pineapple chunks (1-inch)
1 1/2 cups whole milk
1 vanilla bean, split lengthwise
1/2 cup tequila or rum
3 large eggs

3 large egg yolks
2/3 cup sugar
2 tbsp. all-purpose flour
2 tbsp. heavy cream

Preheat the oven to 400°F. Butter a 10-inch shallow baking or soufflé dish. Scatter the pineapple chunks over the bottom. Bake until the pineapple caramelizes, about 20 minutes. Remove from the oven and reduce the temperature to 350°F.

Heat the milk in a medium saucepan over medium heat. Scrape the vanilla seeds into the milk, then add the vanilla bean. Bring to a simmer. Remove from the heat and let steep 15 minutes. Remove the vanilla bean and whisk in the tequila or rum. In a medium bowl, whisk the eggs, egg yolks, sugar, flour, and cream until smooth. Gradually whisk in the hot milk. Pour the mixture over the pineapple. Bake until a knife inserted in the center comes out clean, about 30 minutes. Serve warm or at room temperature, spooned into bowls.

Serves 8

mexican chocolate ice cream

see variations page 251

Made with sugar, almonds, and cinnamon, each small disk of Mexican chocolate has most of the flavorings you need to make this ice cream.

8 large egg yolks
1 cup sugar
2 cups milk, heated until hot
1 lb. Mexican chocolate, grated

1 tsp. vanilla extract
grated chocolate and toasted sliced almonds,
   to garnish

In a large saucepan, whisk the egg yolks and sugar together until light yellow, about 3–5 minutes. Slowly whisk in half of the hot milk until well blended. Place the saucepan over medium-high heat and whisk in the remaining hot milk. Cook, whisking occasionally, until the mixture coats the back of a spoon, about 10 minutes. Remove from the heat, add the grated chocolate and vanilla, and whisk to blend and melt the chocolate. When the mixture is smooth, let cool to room temperature.

Pour the mixture into an ice cream maker and freeze according to manufacturer's directions. To serve, spoon the ice cream into dishes and garnish with grated chocolate and almonds.

Serves 8

capirotada

see variations page 252

This Mexican bread pudding features the caramel flavor of piloncillo or Mexican brown sugar. Capirotada means "a little bit of everything," from leftover bread to sugar, nuts, spices, fruits, and cheese.

1 cup firmly packed, crumbled piloncillo or light
    brown sugar
1 cup water
2 cinnamon sticks
1 tbsp. freshly grated orange zest

3 cups cubed bread, toasted
1/2 cup toasted pine nuts
1/2 cup toasted, slivered almonds
1 cup raisins or dried mango
8 oz. Monterey Jack cheese, cubed

Preheat the oven to 350°F. Grease the inside of a 9x13-inch baking dish and set aside. In a saucepan, bring the piloncillo, water, and cinnamon to a boil over medium-high heat. Cook until slightly thickened, about 5 minutes. Remove from the heat and stir the orange zest into the syrup. Arrange the bread cubes in the prepared baking dish and top them with the pine nuts, almonds, raisins, and cheese. Pour the piloncillo syrup over the bread cubes and toss with a fork to blend. Bake, covered, for 25 minutes. Uncover and bake for 5 minutes more.

Serves 8–10

cajeta chocolate cake

see variations page 253

This rich, moist version of tres leches (three milks) cake has a cajeta (caramel) topping.

for the cajeta
1 (12 1/2-oz) can evaporated
    goat's milk
1 cup sugar
2 tbsp. butter
1 tsp. vanilla extract
salt to taste

for the cake
1 (18 1/4-oz.) package devil's
    food cake mix
1 (14-oz.) can sweetened
    condensed milk
1 (12-oz.) can evaporated milk
1/2 cup milk

8 oz. package cream cheese at
    room temperature
5 large eggs
1 tsp. vanilla extract

Stir the milk, sugar, and butter together in a large saucepan over high heat. Bring to a boil. Cook, whisking often, for 10 minutes. Continue cooking and whisking constantly until the mixture begins to turn medium-brown, about 10 more minutes. Remove from the heat and stir in the vanilla. The sauce should flow from a spoon and will thicken as it cools. After the Cajeta cools, taste and add a little salt if necessary. Preheat oven to 350°F. Grease and flour a large Bundt pan. Pour the Cajeta into the prepared pan. Prepare the cake mix according to package directions. Pour the cake batter on top of the Cajeta. In a blender or food processor, combine the three milks with the cream cheese, eggs, and vanilla. Pour the mixture into the pan so it covers the top of the cake batter. Cover the Bundt pan with foil and place in a larger baking pan. Add enough hot water to reach 2 inches up the sides of the Bundt pan. Bake, covered, for 2 hours or until a toothpick inserted near the center comes out clean. Remove from the oven and let cool, then remove the foil. Invert the cake onto a large plate or serving dish so the Cajeta drips down the sides of the cake. Refrigerate at least 1 hour before serving.

Serves 12–16

bunuelos

see base recipe page 231

sweet orange bunuelos
Replace the cinnamon with 2 tablespoons orange zest.

chile-spice bunuelos
Prepare the basic recipe, adding 1 teaspoon ground chipotle or ancho chile to the cinnamon sugar.

sweet bunuelos chips
On a flat surface, stack 4 tortillas on top of each other, making 3 stacks of tortillas. Using a pizza wheel or a sharp knife, slice each tortilla stack into 8 triangles. Fry the triangles in batches until golden brown and crisp, about 30–60 seconds. Remove with a slotted spoon, drain on paper towels, and sprinkle with cinnamon sugar.

torta de bunuelos
Prepare the basic recipe. In a blender or food processor, process 2 cups queso fresco or farmer's cheese with 2 cups heavy cream and 1 teaspoon vanilla extract until somewhat smooth. Thinly spread 1 prepared bunuelo with 3 tablespoons of this mixture, then stack another bunuelo on top. Repeat the process until all the filling is used and you have a big stack of bunuelos. Let rest to slightly soften, then cut into wedges to serve.

variations

mexican wedding cookies

see base recipe page 232

walnut wedding cookies
Prepare the basic recipe, using walnuts in place of almonds.

pecan wedding cookies
Prepare the basic recipe, using pecans in place of almonds.

mexican wedding sandwich cookies
Prepare the basic recipe. Spread a teaspoon of prepared cajeta (page 244) or canned dulce de leche on the bottom of one cookie, then place the bottom of a second cookie on the filling to sandwich the two together.

lemon-almond wedding cookies
Prepare the basic recipe, adding 1 teaspoon lemon zest to the cookie dough before forming balls.

variations

mango ice cream

see base recipe page 234

papaya ice cream
Prepare the basic recipe, using 4 cups fresh, ripe papayas in place of
mangoes.

guava ice cream
Prepare the basic recipe, using 4 cups fresh and ripe or canned guavas in
place of mangoes.

banana ice cream
Prepare the basic recipe, using 4 cups fresh, ripe bananas in place
of mangoes.

a trio of mexican ice creams
Prepare three of the ice creams and serve a scoop of each on each
dessert plate.

avocado ice cream
Prepare the basic recipe, using 3 ripe avocados, pitted and chopped, in place
of the mangoes.

variations

mexican rice pudding

see base recipe page 237

mexican rice pudding with fresh berries
Prepare the basic recipe, using 1 cup fresh berries (not soaked in water) in place of the dried fruit.

mexican rice pudding with roasted pineapple
Prepare the basic recipe, using roasted pineapple chunks in place of the dried fruit. To prepare the pineapple, toss 1 cup fresh pineapple chunks with 1 tablespoon brown sugar and roast at 450°F for 15 minutes.

mexican rice pudding with mexican chocolate sauce
Prepare the basic recipe. To make the sauce, combine a 3.3-oz. disk of Mexican chocolate with 1/2 cup heavy cream in a medium saucepan over low heat, stirring until the chocolate melts. Spoon the sauce over each serving of rice pudding.

breakfast rice pudding
Prepare the basic recipe. Chill the pudding overnight. In the morning, place a spoonful in a bowl and top with fresh berries, toasted nuts, and a dollop of crèma.

passion fruit sorbet

see base recipe page 239

coconut sorbet
Prepare the basic recipe, using frozen coconut pulp in place of passion fruit.

tropical fruit sorbetti
Prepare both passion fruit and coconut sorbets and serve together in a glass dish, garnished with mint leaves.

papaya sorbet
Prepare the basic recipe, using frozen papaya pulp in place of passion fruit.

guava & crème fraîche sorbet
Prepare the basic recipe, using frozen guava pulp in place of passion fruit and adding 1 cup crème fraîche (prepared or mix 1/2 cup heavy cream with 1/2 cup sour cream or crèma).

tequila and passion fruit slush
Prepare the basic recipe. When frozen, add 2 fl.oz tequila to 1 scoop passion fruit sorbet and blend. Serve immediately in a tall glass.

hacienda-style flan

see base recipe page 240

hacienda-style pumpkin flan
Prepare the basic recipe, using fresh pumpkin cubes in place of pineapple.

hacienda-style squash flan
Prepare the basic recipe, using cubes of fresh acorn or butternut squash in place of pineapple.

hacienda-style coconut flan
Prepare the basic recipe, using 2 cups grated fresh coconut in place of pineapple. Bake the coconut until it is lightly browned, about 10–15 minutes, then proceed with the recipe.

hacienda-style papaya flan
Prepare the basic recipe, using cubes of fresh, ripe papaya in place of pineapple.

variations

mexican chocolate ice cream

see base recipe page 241

mexican chipotle-chocolate ice cream
Prepare the basic recipe, adding 1 teaspoon ground dried chipotle with
the vanilla.

mexican chocolate-almond ice cream
Prepare the basic recipe, adding 1 cup toasted, sliced almonds with
the vanilla.

easy mexican chocolate chip ice cream
Grate 8 ounces Mexican chocolate. Soften 1 quart vanilla ice cream. In a
bowl, blend the chocolate with the softened ice cream. Cover and freeze.

mexican coffee & chocolate ice cream
Prepare the basic recipe, adding 1/4 cup ground Mexican coffee to the milk
before heating it. Set coffee-flavored milk aside to steep for 15 minutes. Line
a sieve with cheesecloth and strain the milk into a bowl. Discard the coffee
grounds, and proceed with the recipe.

variations

capirotada

see base recipe page 242

capirotada with cajeta
Prepare the basic recipe. Warm 1 recipe cajeta (page 244) in a medium saucepan over low heat, stirring until melted. Spoon the sauce over each serving of bread pudding.

capirotada with blueberries
Prepare the basic recipe, using 1 cup fresh blueberries in place of raisins.

capirotada with sweet mango cream
Prepare the basic recipe. Drizzle each serving with sweet mango cream (page 27).

capirotada french toast
Prepare the basic recipe, dividing the mixture between 2 (5x9-inch) loaf pans. Bake and allow to cool. Whisk 5 large eggs with 1 tablespoon vanilla in a shallow bowl. Slice each loaf of capirotada into 8 slices. Melt 4 tablespoons butter in a large skillet over medium-high heat. Dip both sides of each slice into the egg mixture, then shallow-fry until golden on each side, about 4 minutes. To serve, dust each slice with confectioners' sugar.

cajeta chocolate cake

see base recipe page 244

cajeta spice cake
Prepare the basic recipe, using spice cake mix in place of devil's food.

pantry cajeta cake
Prepare the basic recipe, using canned dulce de leche in place of homemade cajeta.

mexican chocolate cake
Prepare the basic recipe, omitting the cajeta. After baking, cooling, and inverting the cake onto a platter, drizzle warm Mexican chocolate sauce (page 248) over the cake.

cajeta orange cake
Prepare the basic recipe, using yellow cake mix in place of devil's food. Add 1 tablespoon freshly grated orange zest to the cake batter.

drinks

What would drinks be today without Mexico's
contributions of chocolate, vanilla, tequila, and
coffee? From cocktails to hot chocolate, Mexican
ingredients put the "ole" at the beginning and end
of a meal.

world's best margarita

see variations page 271

Made from the blue agave plant that is native to the desert region of western Mexico, tequila evolved from a fermented beverage drunk by the Aztecs. When the Spanish conquistadors ran out of brandy after they landed in 1521, they created tequila, the first distilled beverage in the New World. In Mexico, a margarita is made with native Key limes, the smaller, thinner-skinned version of the more common Persian lime. Use the best-quality tequila for the best flavor.

1 cup fresh lime juice
1 cup Grand Marnier or Triple Sec
2 cups tequila
wedges of fresh lime
salt, optional

Pour the lime juice, Grand Marnier, and tequila in a large pitcher, and stir. Use a wedge of lime to wipe the rim of each margarita glass, then dip each rim into a saucer of salt, if you like.

Choose one of several ways of serving: Stir the margarita mixture with crushed ice, then strain into a glass for a straight margarita. Pour the mixture into a glass full of crushed ice for a margarita on the rocks. Freeze the margarita mixture for at least 8 hours or until just slushy, then pour or spoon into glasses.

Serves 20

mexican mojito

see variations page 272

While the original Cuban mojito is based on rum, the Mexican mojito uses tequila and Key limes for more flavor.

10 fresh mint leaves, plus 1 sprig for garnish
juice of 2 Persian or 4 Key limes
1/3 cup water
2 tbsp. superfine sugar
1 cup crushed ice
1 1/2 oz. tequila

Tear the mint leaves in half and place them in a cocktail shaker. Using a muddler or the end of a wooden spoon, mash the leaves until bruised and fragrant. Add the lime juice, water, sugar, ice, and tequila. Cover the shaker and shake briskly. Pour into a tall glass and garnish with a mint sprig.

Serves 1

michelada

see variations page 273

The Michelada beer cocktail, slang for "my cold beer," originated in northern Mexico in the 1940s as a simple combination of beer, salt, lime, and ice. Now, each bar has its own take.

1 wedge fresh lime
coarse kosher or flake salt
1 (12-oz.) bottle Mexican beer, such as Tecate or
   Dos Equis, very cold

1/4 cup fresh lime juice
1 tsp. Worcestershire sauce
1-2 dashes bottled hot sauce

Use the wedge of lime to wipe the rim of a glass with juice, then dip the rim into a saucer of salt. Fill the glass halfway with ice. Pour in the beer, lime juice, Worcestershire, and hot sauce. Stir with a spoon. Drink, then top off with the rest of the beer as needed.

Serves 1

summer fruit coolers

see variations page 274

Street vendors in Mexican towns often serve a refreshing drink called agua fresca, based on fruit juices and purées as well as the tart hibiscus or Jamaica flower, tropical tamarind, and even fresh cucumber. In a rainbow of colors, these drinks are sometimes served from barrel-shaped glass jars called vitroleros.

2 cups seeded, peeled, and coarsely chopped
    cantaloupe or honeydew melon
2-4 tbsp. sugar
2-4 tbsp. fresh lime juice
2 cups water

In a blender, purée the fruit. Season to taste with sugar and lime juice until flavorful and tangy. Stir the fruit mixture and water together in a pitcher and serve over ice.

Serves 4

sangrita with a tequila chaser

see variations page 275

Served in tall frosty glasses, sangrita — with its accompanying shot of tequila — is a bracing cure for a hangover or a way to wake up a sleepy afternoon. It's like a deconstructed Bloody Mary, only more citrus-flavored, and with a green onion as a swizzle stick.

1 cup tomato juice
2 cups fresh orange juice
1/2 cup fresh lime juice
1/4 tsp. bottled hot sauce
4 green onions, trimmed slightly on both ends
4 shots tequila in individual shot glasses

Combine the juices and hot sauce in a large pitcher. Stir to blend. Pour into frosty glasses over ice. Add a green onion to each glass. Serve each glass with a shot glass of tequila.

Serves 4

prickly pear lemonade

see variations page 276

Prickly pear is the dark red fruit of a cactus that grows in the deserts of northern and western Mexico. It has a flavor similar to kiwi and is delicious in this rosy-colored take on lemonade.

4 cups water
juice of 6 lemons, plus 1 sliced lemon for
    garnish

1/2 cup prickly pear juice or syrup
2/3 cup sugar

In a large pitcher, stir the water, lemon juice, prickly pear juice, and sugar together until the sugar dissolves. To serve, pour over ice in a tall glass and garnish with a lemon slice.

Serves 6

sangria

see variations page 277

Brought from Spain to Mexico, refreshing sangria is usually served in earthenware or glass pitchers with antojitos or appetizers.

2 cups fresh orange juice
1/2 cup Grand Marnier or Triple Sec
1 bottle (750 ml) light red or rosé wine
1/4 cup sugar
1 orange, thinly sliced
1 lime, thinly sliced

Combine all ingredients in a large pitcher and refrigerate until well chilled. Serve over ice, if desired.

Serves 4–6

tequila hot toddy

see variations page 278

Cold weather, runny nose, bad day — these are all good reasons to make a tequila hot toddy for yourself or someone you love.

2 tbsp. tequila
2 tbsp. honey
1 lemon slice

cinnamon stick (optional)
hot water

Place the tequila, honey, lemon slice, and cinnamon stick in a coffee mug. Add hot water and use the cinnamon stick to muddle the lemon and stir the ingredients together. Drink while it's hot.

Serves 1

mexican coffee

see variations page 279

Coffee came to Mexico from the Antilles and has been cultivated in the highlands since the late 18th century. Known as café de olla — after the earthenware pot in which it is traditionally brewed — this coffee also tastes wonderful when made in a drip coffeemaker. Look for Mexican coffee varieties with "SHG" on the package for "strictly high grown" coffee beans grown in the highest altitude, which contributes to their robust flavor.

1/2 cup ground Mexican coffee
1 (3-inch) cinnamon stick, broken in half
1 small (about 3-oz.) cone piloncillo, broken into pieces,
    or 4 tbsp. firmly packed dark brown sugar
4 cups water

Place the coffee, cinnamon stick pieces, and piloncillo in a coffee filter. Place the water in the drip coffee pot. Brew, then pour into cups to serve.

Serves 4-6

champurrado

see variations page 280

A warm, spicy, and milky drink usually served with bunuelos (page 231), champurrado is a favorite during the holiday season. It's thickened with the same instant corn flour used to make corn tortillas.

2 cups warm water
1/2 cup masa harina or instant corn masa
2 cups milk
1 (3.3-oz.) disk Mexican chocolate, finely
   chopped

1 (3-oz.) piloncillo cone, chopped
1/4 tsp. ground anise seed or cinnamon

Combine the water and masa harina in a bowl and whisk until somewhat thickened. Set aside.

Combine the milk, chocolate, and piloncillo in a large saucepan over medium-high heat and stir until steamy and the chocolate and piloncillo have melted; do not boil. Whisk in the masa mixture and cook, stirring, for a few minutes more until thickened. Remove from the heat, add the ground anise seed, and place the bulbous end of the molinillo in the hot mixture. Place the molinillo handle between your palms and rotate to froth the mixture (or use a wire whisk). Pour into mugs to serve. Strain through a sieve before serving, if you like.

Serves 4–6

mexican hot chocolate

see variations page 281

According to ancient Toltec legend, the god Quetzalcoatl brought seeds of the cacao tree to Earth. These seeds produced one of Mexico's best-known gifts to the food world: chocolate. Grocery stores with a range of Mexican products offer packages of Mexican chocolate – small disks of semisweet chocolate mixed with cinnamon, sugar, and ground almonds. Although this is not quite the dark chocolate beverage that the Aztec ruler Montezuma drank, Mexican hot chocolate is creamy and mildly spicy. To be really authentic, froth it with a molinillo, a turned wood stirrer that you hold between your palms and rotate.

4 cups whole milk
1 (3.3-oz.) disk Mexican chocolate,
    finely chopped

Heat the milk and chocolate in a large saucepan until steamy and the chocolate has melted; do not boil. Remove from the heat and place the bulbous end of the molinillo in the hot chocolate. Place the molinillo handle between your palms and rotate to froth the chocolate (or use a wire whisk). Pour into mugs to serve.

Serves 4–6

variations

world's best margarita

see base recipe page 255

world's best pomegranate margarita
Prepare the basic recipe, using 1/2 cup pomegranate juice in place of
1/2 cup of the lime juice.

world's best mango margarita
Prepare the basic recipe, using 1/2 cup mango juice in place of 1/2 cup of
the lime juice.

world's best passion fruit margarita
Prepare the basic recipe, using 1/2 cup frozen and thawed passion fruit
purée in place of 1/2 cup of the lime juice.

world's best prickly pear margarita
Prepare the basic recipe, using 1/2 cup frozen and thawed prickly pear purée
in place of 1/2 cup of the lime juice.

variations

mexican mojito

see base recipe page 256

mango mojito
Prepare the basic recipe, using mango nectar in place of water.

lemongrass mojito
Prepare the basic recipe, adding 2 fresh lemongrass stalks about 4 inches long. Bruise them along with the mint leaves.

blackberry mojito
Prepare the basic recipe, using blackberry juice in place of water.

pineapple mojito
Prepare the basic recipe, using pineapple juice in place of water. Garnish with a spear of fresh pineapple.

michelada

see base recipe page 257

macho michelada
Prepare the basic recipe. Serve with a shot of tequila as a chaser.

tex-mex michelada
Fill a large mug with ice, pour light lager beer over it, and squeeze in fresh lime juice to taste.

mucho gusto michelada
Do not salt the rim. Prepare the basic recipe, using bottled Maggi seasoning in place of Worcestershire sauce and adding 1/4 teaspoon celery salt and 1/4 teaspoon adobo seasoning to the glass.

mexico city michelada
Prepare the basic recipe, adding 1 cup tomato juice to the lime juice.

variations

summer fruit coolers

see base recipe page 258

watermelon agua fresca
Prepare the basic recipe, using watermelon in place of the cantaloupe
or honeydew.

mango agua fresca
Prepare the basic recipe, using mango in place of the cantaloupe
or honeydew.

strawberry agua fresca
Prepare the basic recipe, using hulled fresh strawberries in place of the
cantaloupe or honeydew.

tamarind agua fresca
Prepare the basic recipe, using 2 cups tamarind pulp in place of the
cantaloupe or honeydew. Strain the tamarind mixture through a sieve before
adding to the water.

sangrita with a tequila chaser

see base recipe page 260

chipotle sangrita
Prepare the basic recipe, using 1/2 cup bottled chipotle marinade in place of bottled hot pepper sauce.

spicy sangrita
Prepare the basic recipe, using spicy V-8 or a spicy tomato juice in place of plain tomato juice and 1/2 cup bottled chipotle marinade in place of bottled hot pepper sauce.

sangrita cocktail
Prepare the basic recipe, stirring the shot of tequila into the drink before serving.

virgin sangrita
Prepare the basic recipe, omitting the tequila chaser.

variations

prickly pear lemonade

see base recipe page 262

prickly pear & mango lemonade
Prepare the basic recipe, adding 1 cup mango nectar.

lemongrass lemonade
Prepare the basic recipe, omitting the prickly pear juice. Place the water and sugar in a saucepan with 2 (4-inch) stalks of fresh lemongrass and bring to a boil. Remove from the heat and let steep for 30 minutes or until just warm. Stir in the lemon juice and pour over ice in a tall glass.

mexican hibiscus flower lemonade
Prepare the basic recipe, omitting the prickly pear juice. Place the water and sugar in a saucepan with 3 hibiscus flower teabags and bring to a boil. Remove from the heat and let steep for 30 minutes or until just warm. Stir in the lemon juice and pour over ice in a tall glass.

hot prickly pear lemonade
Prepare the basic recipe, combining all ingredients in a saucepan over medium-high heat until hot. Serve in mugs.

variations

sangria

see base recipe page 263

white sangria
Prepare the basic recipe, using Chardonnay or another dry white wine in place of red or rosé.

sangria roja
Prepare the basic recipe, using pomegranate juice in place of orange juice and pomegranate seeds in place of orange slices.

tropical sangria
Prepare the basic recipe, using Chardonnay or another dry white wine in place of red or rosé wine and mango nectar in place of orange juice.

sparkling sangria
Prepare the basic recipe, using a cold, sparkling white wine in place of red or rosé. Do not chill, but serve right away over ice.

variations

tequila hot toddy

see base recipe page 265

tequila hot toddy with lime
Prepare the basic recipe, using a wedge of fresh lime in place of the lemon slice.

rum hot toddy
Prepare the basic recipe, using dark rum in place of tequila.

prickly pear hot toddy
Heat 1 cup of prickly pear lemonade (page 276), add 2 tablespoons tequila, and serve hot in a coffee mug.

really bad day hot toddy
Prepare the basic recipe, using 4 tablespoons tequila.

virgin toddy
Prepare the basic recipe, using 2 fl oz. apple cider vinegar in place of the tequila.

variations

mexican coffee

see base recipe page 266

spiced mexican coffee
Prepare the basic recipe, adding 1/2 teaspoon ground cinnamon and
1/2 teaspoon ground chipotle to the coffee grounds.

after-dinner mexican coffee
Prepare the basic recipe, adding 1-2 tablespoons of coffee-flavored liqueur
to each cup before pouring in the coffee.

iced mexican coffee
Prepare the basic recipe, letting the coffee cool. Fill 4 large glasses with ice.
Pour 1 tablespoon of half-and-half in each glass. Pour the coffee into the
glasses and stir to blend.

mexican coffee affogatto
Prepare the basic recipe. To make this sundae, put 2 scoops of vanilla or
coffee ice cream in each of 4 bowls. Pour hot coffee over the ice cream
and serve.

mexican coffee with almond liqueur
Prepare the basic recipe, adding a shot of Mexican almond liqueur to each
cup just before serving.

variations

champurrado

see base recipe page 268

spiced champurrado
Prepare the basic recipe, adding 1/2 teaspoon ground cinnamon and
1/2 teaspoon ground dried chipotle in place of the 1/4 teaspoon anise seed.

after-dinner champurrado
Prepare the basic recipe. To serve, add a shot of chocolate liqueur to each
mug and top with whipped cream.

orange champurrado
Prepare the basic recipe, adding 1 tablespoon grated orange zest with the
anise seed.

las posadas champurrado
For the *las posadas* tradition at Christmas serve champurrado in little cups
accompanied by a small cookie to friends who stop by.

variations

mexican hot chocolate

see base recipe page 270

mexican hot chocolate with tequila
Prepare the basic recipe, adding a shot of tequila to each mug of hot chocolate.

mexican hot chocolate coffee
Brew 8 cups of coffee. Place 1 tablespoon of crumbled Mexican chocolate in
the bottom of each coffee mug and pour in the hot coffee. Stir to blend. Add
cream or sugar if desired.

mexican hot white chocolate drink
Prepare the basic recipe, using 3 ounces white chocolate chips, 3 tablespoons
ground almonds, 1 tablespoon sugar, and 2 teaspoons ground cinnamon in
place of the Mexican chocolate.

mexican hot chocolate sundae
Prepare the basic recipe and pour 1/2 cup hot chocolate over a scoop of vanilla
ice cream. Serve immediately.

hot chocolate with coffee liqueur
Prepare the basic recipe adding a shot of coffee liqueur to each mug of
hot chocolate.

index